MAKE,
BAKE,
COOKIES
the recipe book

MAKE, BAKE, COOKIES

the recipe book

EASY AND INDULGENT TREATS
TO FILL UP YOUR COOKIE JAR

LOVE FOOD™

CONTENTS

Baked To Perfection

Every home should have a well-stocked jar of cookies ready and waiting to be dipped into! Cookies are easy and enjoyable to make and they are great to share over a mid-morning coffee or afternoon cup of tea. Since they're made in individual servings, they're perfectly portion-sized (although it can be difficult to stop after eating just one!) and there's no hassle with cutting and serving.

The beauty of home-made cookies is that you can customize them for any occasion or celebration. Using shaped cookie cutters or adding simple icings and decorations, you can create artistic masterpieces that look just as good as they taste.

No matter what flavour of cookie you choose or how you decide to adorn them, making delicious cookies is a breeze and decorating them is much easier than you might imagine. Just follow the simple recipes, helpful tips and step-by-step decorating instructions in this book and you'll soon be whipping up batches of perfectly baked cookies.

Once you've mastered the basic recipes and techniques, the sky's the limit! All you need is a dash of imagination and you'll be able to create cookies to suit any occasion. Happy baking, decorating and, of course, devouring!

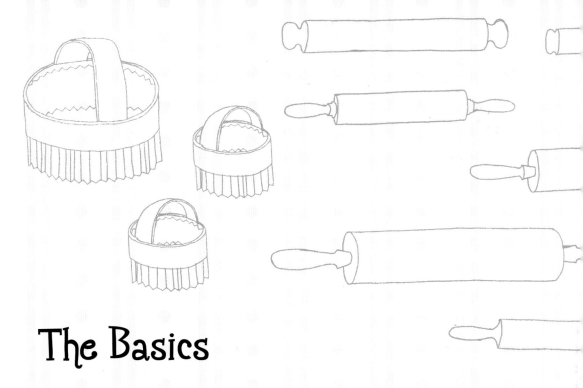

The Basics

Whether they're soft and chewy, crisp and crumbly, covered in fancy icing or filled with special ingredients, most of the cookies in this book are either cut-out, sliced, drop or piped cookies.

Cut-out cookies
These cookies are defined by their cut shapes, created using a cookie cutter. The dough is often chilled before being rolled out, and again before it is baked – this helps the cookies to keep their shape and minimizes spreading in the oven.

Sliced cookies
As the name suggests, sliced cookies are created when dough is rolled into a long log shape and sliced to create the individual cookies.

Drop cookies
Drop cookies have a more textured, wetter dough than other varieties, and often include ingredients like nuts or chocolate chips. The dough is spooned onto baking sheets before baking.

Piped cookies
Piped cookies are made by spooning the soft cookie dough into a piping bag fitted with a large nozzle and by piping it in various shapes onto the baking sheets. Alternatively, a cookie press – which looks a bit like a caulking gun – may be used. This can be fitted with discs of varying designs to create decoratively shaped cookies.

The Star Ingredients

Fat, sugar, eggs and flour are the basic ingredients for most cookie recipes, so are useful ingredients to have to hand if you're serious about getting into cookie making!

Fat

Butter is the ideal fat for making cookies, giving them a rich flavour that margarine cannot match. Unsalted butter is always best for sweet baking. However, if you prefer to use margarine, make sure to use one that is described on the packet as suitable for baking.

Sugar

Caster sugar is usually recommended because it dissolves more easily than granulated sugar. Brown sugar or muscovado sugar is used in some recipes to give a richer flavour. Icing sugar is powdery and used to make icings and buttercream fillings. It can also be dusted over cookies to decorate them.

Eggs

Unless otherwise stated, the size of the eggs used in the recipes is medium. If possible, use eggs at room temperature because cold eggs may cause curdling and will result in a less soft mixture.

Flour

The flour used in the recipes may be plain or self-raising. Should you need self-raising flour but only have plain, sift 2½ teaspoons of baking powder into every 225 g/8 oz plain flour. It is not necessary to sift flour unless you are combining several dry ingredients.

Additional ingredients, such as flavouring extracts, dried fruits, nuts and chocolate, will add flavour and texture and are what turn a basic cookie into something quite extraordinary!

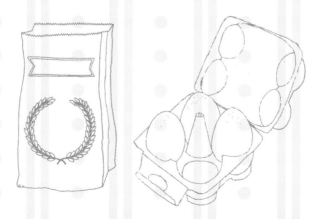

Essential Equipment

You won't need loads of expensive equipment or specialist cooking tools to make cookies but there are a few essentials.

Baking sheets
It is worth investing in a few good-quality baking sheets as cheaper ones have a tendency to buckle in the oven and may not distribute heat evenly. It may sound obvious, but do check the dimensions of your oven before buying baking sheets.

Baking paper
Baking paper has a shiny, non-stick surface. Its main use is to line baking sheets to prevent cookies from sticking to them, but it's also useful when rolling out cookie dough – by placing the dough between two sheets of baking paper you eliminate the need to add additional flour and thus avoid upsetting the balance of ingredients. Baking paper can also be used to make paper piping bags (see page 11) and to place decorated cookies on to dry.

Electric mixer
An electric mixer is useful for whisking and beating mixtures together but, failing this, use a balloon whisk for whisking and a wooden spoon for creaming.

Rolling pin
This is a useful piece of kit if you wish to make rolled cookies, but there are plenty of cookies you can still make if you don't have one.

Cookie cutters
Again, these are for use with rolled cookies only and are not strictly essential, but there is such a range of shapes and sizes available that you might be tempted to buy some anyway! If you don't have a cookie cutter in the desired shape, it's easy to make a template out of cardboard. Simply place the template on top of the rolled cookie dough and cut around it with a small, sharp knife.

Wire racks
Wire racks are handy for cooling your cookies. The design allows air to circulate around the cookies, preventing them from becoming soggy.

Piping bags and nozzles
There are plenty of ways to ice and decorate cookies without needing a piping bag or nozzle, but you might want to consider investing in a small set if you want to try the more elaborate designs in this book.

Icing Masterclass

Icing is the final flourish when it comes to your home-baked cookies, and it can add colour and flavour to your baking. Knowing which icing is best for your latest batch of baking is essential if you want to add the 'wow factor'.

Royal icing

Made with icing sugar, egg whites (or egg white powder) and water (or lemon juice), this is the go-to icing for creating works of art on your cookies. It can be used to pipe the outline of the desired shape on a cookie, and then watered down slightly to fill or 'flood' the area inside the outline to make a solid shape. Once set, royal icing gives a hard, smooth surface that's perfect for decorating with edible markers or food colouring 'paint'. You can, of course, create coloured royal icing and, because of its long setting time, it's possible to create all sorts of impressive effects (like spots or feathering) just by combining a mixture of colours.

Glacé icing

The simplest icing of all – glacé icing is basically a mixture of icing sugar and water (and food colouring, if desired). It can be mixed to a thin consistency for a light glaze on a cookie, or beaten until thick and smooth for more controlled decorations. Glacé icing is great for attaching other decorations to your cookies, or simply for adding a burst of sweetness to your baking.

Fondant icing

The appeal of fondant icing (or sugar paste) is that it can be coloured, rolled, cut, moulded and shaped into all sorts of designs to give a polished look to your cookies. Some people aren't keen on the taste of fondant, but it can be flavoured using concentrated flavouring oils or extracts.

There's no need to go to the trouble of making your own fondant because ready-to-roll fondant is readily available. To colour fondant icing yourself, use gel or paste food colouring to achieve vibrant hues without affecting the consistency by adding liquid.

Buttercream frosting

This fluffy frosting is made from butter and icing sugar, beaten until it's soft and light. Buttercream can be spread with a spatula or piped and is ideal as a filling for sandwich cookies.

Piping Perfection

Piping bags, usually used in conjunction with piping nozzles, are extremely handy for piping icing or even, in the case of piped cookies, for piping the cookie mixture itself. Whether you choose to use reusable or disposable piping bags, make sure to suit the size of the bag to the job. For piping cookie mixture or buttercream, use large bags that allow plenty of room for filling. For royal or glacé icing, use a small or medium-sized bag.

Paper piping bags are handy if you have a number of different-coloured icings on the go at one time. To make a small paper piping bag, take a 25-cm/10-inch square of baking paper. Fold it diagonally in half, then hold the two points at each end of the long edge. Curl one point over to meet the centre point, making a cone shape, then curl the other point over so that all three points meet. Fold the points over a couple of times to secure the cone. Snip off the end and use with or without a piping nozzle. You can also use a heavy-duty plastic food bag as a piping bag by snipping off the corner and inserting a piping nozzle, if desired.

To fill a piping bag, cut off about 1 cm/½ inch from the tip and insert your piping nozzle. Fold the sides down over your hand (alternatively, you can place the bag in a tall glass or jug, folding the bag down over the sides) and, using the other hand, scoop in the icing or cookie mixture using a spatula. Do not over-fill the bag – you need to leave enough space at the top to twist it tightly closed. To use, gently squeeze the bag from the top and move the nozzle to create the desired shape or outline.

Piping nozzles come in dozens of shapes and sizes. You can buy them separately or in sets. A fine plain nozzle will come in handy if you wish to decorate your cookies with royal icing, whilst larger plain or shaped nozzles will be useful for making piped cookies or creating decorative effects with buttercream.

The Secrets To Success

There's something extra-special about a home-baked cookie – nothing beats eating still-warm treats, fresh from the oven and made by your own fair hand. To many, baking at home is a daunting prospect, but it's easy! As long as you put in the necessary preparation work beforehand and exercise patience while working through the recipe, you will be richly rewarded by the results.

Before
• Prepare your kitchen by clearing work surfaces and getting out any equipment you may need.

• Check that you have all the ingredients for the recipe you want. There is nothing worse than finding out that you've run out of something halfway through baking.

• Unless otherwise instructed, remove your eggs and butter from the refrigerator about an hour before you begin. This allows the eggs to come up to room temperature and the butter to soften.

• Read the recipes – all the way through!

• Line or grease any baking sheets as per the recipe.

• Preheat the oven for 10–15 minutes. If you have a fan-assisted oven, reduce the temperature according to the manufacturer's instructions.

• Measure out the ingredients carefully and follow either metric or imperial – don't mix the two!

During
• Clean up as you go – wipe down work surfaces, put away ingredients and neatly stack washing up for later.

• Stick to the chilling, cooling or setting times specified – they're there for a reason, and are the perfect excuse for a mid-baking tea break!

• Always place the cookie dough on cold baking sheets to prevent the dough from spreading excessively and browning too much around the edges.

• Space cookies well apart on the baking sheet to allow room for them to spread during cooking – otherwise your cookies may merge together and you could end up with one large cookie!

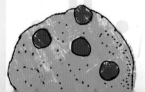

• Don't peek in the oven until the minimum baking time is reached. Opening the door of the oven lets the heat out and may affect the final consistency of your cookies.

After
• Unless otherwise instructed, transfer cookies to a wire rack as soon as they are firm enough to handle. This will allow steam to evaporate and stop your cookies from going soggy.

• Allow cookies to cool completely before storing in airtight containers or decorating.

Storage

Cookies are, of course, at their best when freshly baked. With a few exceptions, most of the cookies in this book will keep well in a cookie jar or other airtight container. The following tips will help, however:

• Always cool cookies completely before storing in airtight containers, otherwise they are liable to stick together.

• Ideally, store baked cookies undecorated – most undecorated cookies will keep in an airtight container for up to a week. Cookies decorated with glacé icing, royal icing or fondant can be stored for up to three days. Cookies frosted with buttercream should be eaten the day they are made.

• Store soft varieties of cookies separately from crisp ones so that they don't all become soft.

• One or two sugar cubes added to a tin of cookies helps to keep them crisp.

• Unfrosted cookies can also be frozen, in a single layer in a sealed container, for up to three months. Ice them while they are still frozen, and then defrost in the refrigerator for several hours. Bring to room temperature before serving.

• The cookie dough for many sliced cookies (for example, the Refrigerator Cookies on page 30) may be stored in the refrigerator or freezer and slices cut off and baked as and when required – very convenient if you fancy a couple of freshly baked cookies in a hurry!

• Most frostings, too, can be refrigerated or frozen. Buttercream can be stored in a tightly covered container in the refrigerator for up to two weeks or in the freezer for six months. Thaw frozen frosting in the refrigerator and beat it with an electric mixer for a minute or two before using.

• Ready-to-roll fondant can be stored indefinitely, wrapped tightly, in a cool, dark place.

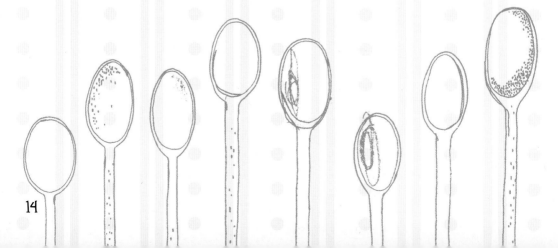

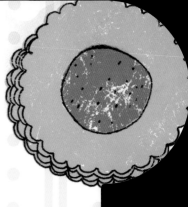

CHAPTER 1

COOKIE JAR FAVOURITES

Chocolate Chip Cookies

makes 8

ingredients

175 g/6 oz plain flour

1 tsp baking powder

125 g/4½ oz margarine,
melted, plus extra
for greasing

85 g/3 oz light muscovado
sugar

55 g/2 oz caster sugar

½ tsp vanilla extract

1 egg, beaten

125 g/4½ oz plain
chocolate chips

1. Preheat the oven to 190°C/375°F/Gas Mark 5. Lightly grease two baking sheets.

2. Sift the flour and baking powder into a large mixing bowl. Add the remaining ingredients and beat until well combined.

3. Place tablespoons of the mixture on the prepared baking sheets, spaced well apart.

4. Bake in the preheated oven for 10–12 minutes, or until golden brown. Leave to cool on the baking sheets for a few minutes, then transfer to a wire rack to cool completely.

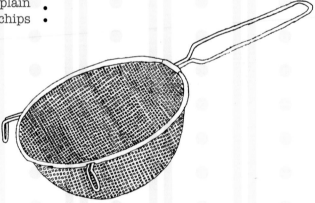

1

2

3

Classic Oat Cookies

makes 30

ingredients

175 g/6 oz unsalted butter,
softened, plus extra
for greasing
275 g/9¾ oz demerara sugar
1 egg, beaten
4 tbsp water
1 tsp vanilla extract
140 g/5 oz plain flour
1 tsp salt
½ tsp bicarbonate of soda
375 g/13 oz rolled oats

1. Preheat the oven to 180°C/350°F/Gas Mark 4.
Lightly grease two large baking sheets.

2. Place the butter and sugar in a large bowl
and beat together until pale and creamy. Beat in
the egg, water and vanilla extract until the mixture
is smooth.

3. Sift the flour, salt and bicarbonate of soda into a
separate bowl and mix in the oats, then gradually
stir the oat mixture into the creamed mixture until
thoroughly combined.

4. Place tablespoonfuls of the mixture on the
prepared baking sheets, spaced well apart.

5. Bake in the preheated oven for 15 minutes, or
until golden brown. Leave to cool on the baking
sheets for a few minutes, then transfer to wire
racks to cool completely.

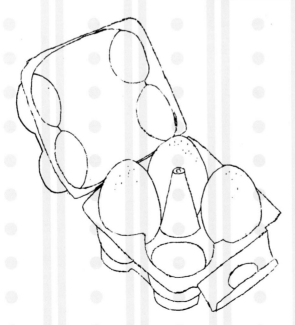

2

3

4

Vanilla Sugar Cookies

makes 24

ingredients

200 g/7 oz unsalted butter, softened

150 g/5½ oz caster sugar

1 large egg

2 tsp vanilla extract

400 g/14 oz plain flour

clear cellophane and colourful ribbons, for wrapping (optional)

1. Line two baking sheets with baking paper.

2. In a large bowl, cream the butter and sugar with an electric mixer until just coming together. Add the egg and vanilla extract and briefly whisk together.

3. Add the flour and use a wooden spoon to mix everything together to make a rough dough. Gather into a ball with your hands, wrap in clingfilm and chill in the refrigerator for at least 10 minutes.

4. Unwrap the dough and roll out between two large sheets of baking paper, turning the dough occasionally until it is an even thickness of about 5 mm/¼ inch. Stamp out about 24 shapes using an 8-cm/3¼-inch star-shaped cutter, re-rolling the dough as necessary.

5. Transfer the cookies to the prepared baking sheets. Chill in the refrigerator for 10 minutes. Meanwhile, preheat the oven to 180°C/350°F/Gas Mark 4.

6. Bake in the preheated oven for 15–18 minutes, or until just turning golden at the edges. Leave to cool on the baking sheets for a few minutes, then transfer to wire racks to cool completely.

7. If you would like to give the cookies as a gift, stack them into piles, wrap in cellophane and tie with ribbon.

3

4

6

Danish Butter Cookies

makes 14

ingredients

115 g/4 oz unsalted butter,
softened

40 g/1½ oz icing sugar, plus
extra for dusting (optional)

125 g/4½ oz plain flour

¼ tsp baking powder

1. Preheat the oven to 190°C/375°F/Gas Mark 5. Line two baking sheets with baking paper.

2. Place the butter in a large bowl and beat with a wooden spoon until very soft and pale. Sift in the icing sugar and beat until smooth. Sift in the flour and baking powder and beat together to form a soft and sticky dough.

3. Spoon the dough into a piping bag fitted with a 1-cm/½-inch fluted nozzle. Pipe 14 wreath shapes onto the prepared baking sheet.

4. Bake in the preheated oven for 10–12 minutes, or until set and pale golden around the edges. Leave to cool on the baking sheets for a few minutes, then transfer to wire racks to cool completely. Dust with icing sugar, if liked.

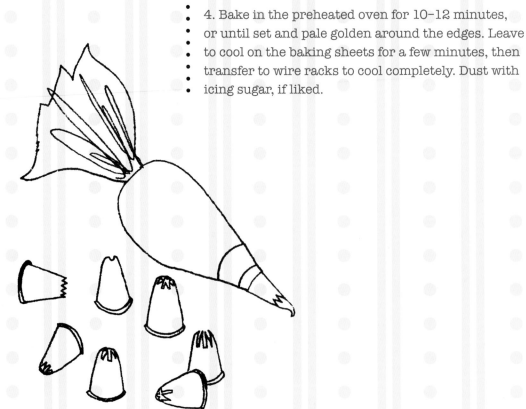

2

3

3

Peanut Butter Cookies

makes 15

ingredients

175 g/6 oz plain flour

½ tsp baking powder

½ tsp salt

225 g/8 oz smooth
peanut butter

115 g/4 oz unsalted butter,
softened, plus extra
for greasing

1¼ tsp vanilla extract

115 g/4 oz soft light
brown sugar

100 g/3½ oz caster sugar

2 eggs

1. Lightly grease two baking sheets. Sift the flour, baking powder and salt into a bowl and set aside.

2. In a separate bowl, beat the peanut butter, butter and vanilla extract until smooth. Beat in the sugars for 1 minute, then beat in the eggs one at a time. Stir in the flour mixture in two batches and mix to form a dough.

3. Shape the dough into a ball, then wrap in clingfilm and chill in the refrigerator for at least 2 hours.

4. Preheat the oven to 180°C/350°F/Gas Mark 4.

5. Unwrap the dough, roll into 4-cm/1½-inch balls and place them on the prepared baking sheets, spaced well apart. Use a fork to flatten each ball, making a criss-cross pattern.

6. Bake in the preheated oven for 15 minutes, or until golden. Leave to cool on the baking sheets for a few minutes, then transfer to a wire rack to cool completely.

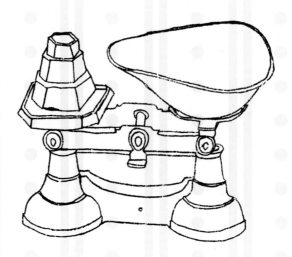

2

3

5

Refrigerator Cookies

makes 56

ingredients

325 g/11½ oz plain flour
2 tbsp cocoa powder
½ tsp bicarbonate of soda
1 tsp ground ginger
½ tsp ground cinnamon
125 ml/4 fl oz treacle
4 tbsp boiling water
115 g/4 oz unsalted butter,
softened
4 tbsp caster sugar
icing sugar, for dusting

1. Sift the flour, cocoa powder, bicarbonate of soda, ginger and cinnamon into a bowl, then set aside. Mix the treacle with the water and set aside.

2. Put the butter into a large bowl and beat with an electric mixer until creamy. Slowly add the caster sugar and continue beating until light and fluffy. Gradually add the flour mixture, alternating it with the treacle mixture to form a soft dough.

3. Scrape equal amounts of the dough onto two pieces of clingfilm and roll into logs, each about 19 cm/7½ inches long and 4 cm/1½ inches thick. Wrap in the clingfilm and put the dough logs in the refrigerator for 2 hours, then transfer to the freezer for at least 2 hours and up to 2 months.

4. When ready to bake, preheat the oven to 180°C/ 350°F/Gas Mark 4. Depending on how many cookies you are baking, line one or two baking sheets with baking paper. Unwrap the dough logs, trim the ends and cut off as many 5-mm/¼-inch slices as you require. Rewrap any unused dough and return to the freezer for another time.

5. Place the dough slices on the prepared baking sheet and bake in the preheated oven for 12 minutes. Leave to cool on the baking sheet for a few minutes, then transfer to a wire rack. Dust with icing sugar and leave to cool completely.

1

2

3

Gingernuts

makes 30

ingredients

350 g/12 oz self-raising flour

pinch of salt

200 g/7 oz caster sugar

1 tbsp ground ginger

1 tsp bicarbonate of soda

125 g/4½ oz unsalted butter, plus extra for greasing

75 g/2¾ oz golden syrup

1 egg, beaten

1 tsp grated orange rind

1. Preheat the oven to 160°C/325°F/Gas Mark 3. Lightly grease two or three baking sheets.

2. Sift the flour, salt, sugar, ginger and bicarbonate of soda into a large bowl and set aside.

3. Heat the butter and golden syrup in a saucepan over a very low heat until the butter has melted. Remove the pan from the heat and leave to cool slightly, then pour the contents onto the dry ingredients.

4. Add the egg and orange rind and mix thoroughly with a wooden spoon to form a dough. Using your hands, carefully shape the dough into 30 equal-sized balls. Place the balls on the prepared baking sheets, spaced well apart, then flatten them slightly with your fingers.

5. Bake in the preheated oven for 15–20 minutes. Leave to cool on the baking sheets for a few minutes, then transfer to wire racks to cool completely.

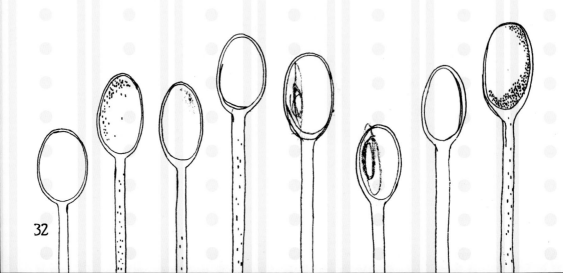

2 3 4

Double Chocolate Whoopie Pies

makes 12

ingredients

200 g/7 oz plain flour

1½ tsp bicarbonate of soda

25 g/1 oz cocoa powder

large pinch of salt

85 g/3 oz unsalted butter, softened

85 g/3 oz white vegetable fat

150 g/5½ oz soft light brown sugar

25 g/1 oz plain chocolate, finely grated

1 large egg, beaten

125 ml/4 fl oz milk

4 tbsp chocolate sprinkles

white chocolate filling

175 g/6 oz white chocolate, broken into pieces

2 tbsp milk

300 ml/10 fl oz double cream

1. Preheat the oven to 180°C/350°F/Gas Mark 4. Line two or three large baking sheets with baking paper.

2. Sift the flour, bicarbonate of soda, cocoa powder and salt into a large bowl and set aside.

3. Place the butter, vegetable fat, sugar and grated chocolate in a separate large bowl and beat with an electric mixer until pale and fluffy. Beat in the egg followed by half the flour mixture, then the milk. Stir in the rest of the flour mixture and mix until thoroughly incorporated.

4. Pipe or spoon 24 mounds of the mixture onto the prepared baking sheets, spaced well apart. Bake in the preheated oven for 10–12 minutes, or until risen and just firm to the touch. Leave to cool on the baking sheets for a few minutes, then transfer to wire racks to cool completely.

5. To make the filling, place the white chocolate and milk in a heatproof bowl set over a saucepan of gently simmering water. Heat until the chocolate has melted, stirring occasionally. Remove from the heat and leave to cool for 30 minutes. Using an electric mixer, whip the cream until holding firm peaks. Fold in the cooled melted chocolate. Cover and chill in the refrigerator for 30–45 minutes, or until firm enough to spread.

6. To assemble, spread or pipe the chocolate filling on the flat side of half the whoopie pies. Top with the remaining whoopie pies. Spread out the chocolate sprinkles on a plate and gently roll the edges of each whoopie pie in the sprinkles to lightly coat.

top tip

For extra rich and chocolatey whoopie pies, use plain chocolate for the filling.

Jam Rings

makes 15

ingredients

225 g/8 oz unsalted butter, softened

140 g/5 oz caster sugar, plus extra for sprinkling

1 egg yolk, lightly beaten

2 tsp vanilla extract

280 g/10 oz plain flour

pinch of salt

1 egg white, lightly beaten

filling

55 g/2 oz unsalted butter, softened

100 g/3½ oz icing sugar

5 tbsp strawberry or raspberry jam

1. Put the butter and caster sugar into a bowl and mix well, then beat in the egg yolk and vanilla extract. Sift the flour and salt into the mixture and mix to form a dough.

2. Halve the dough and shape into two balls, then wrap in clingfilm and chill in the refrigerator for 30–60 minutes.

3. Preheat the oven to 190°C/375°F/Gas Mark 5. Line two baking sheets with baking paper.

4. Unwrap the dough and roll out between two sheets of baking paper. Stamp out cookies with a 7-cm/2¾-inch fluted round cutter and put half of them on one of the prepared baking sheets, spaced well apart. Using a 4-cm/1½-inch plain round cutter, stamp out the centres of the remaining cookies and remove. Put the cookie rings on the other baking sheet, spaced well apart.

5. Bake in the preheated oven for 7 minutes, then brush the cookie rings with the beaten egg white and sprinkle with caster sugar. Bake for a further 5–8 minutes, until light golden brown. Leave to cool on the baking sheets for a few minutes, then transfer to wire racks to cool completely.

6. To make the filling, beat the butter and icing sugar in a bowl. Spread the buttercream over the whole cookies and top with the jam. Place the cookie rings on top and press together.

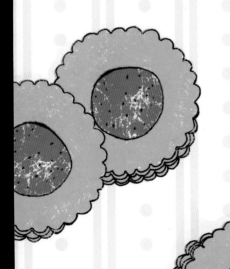

top tip

Add grated lemon rind to
the buttercream and replace
the jam with lemon curd.

Cappuccino Cookies

makes 30

ingredients

2 sachets instant cappuccino

1 tbsp hot water

225 g/8 oz unsalted butter, softened

140 g/5 oz caster sugar

1 egg yolk, lightly beaten

280 g/10 oz plain flour

pinch of salt

topping

175 g/6 oz white chocolate, broken into pieces

cocoa powder, for dusting

1. Empty the cappuccino sachets into a small bowl and stir in the hot, but not boiling, water to make a paste. Put the butter and sugar into a bowl and beat together until pale and creamy, then beat in the egg yolk and cappuccino paste. Sift the flour and salt into the mixture and stir until thoroughly combined.

2. Halve the dough and shape into two balls, then wrap in clingfilm and chill in the refrigerator for 30–60 minutes.

3. Preheat the oven to 190°C/375°F/Gas Mark 5. Line two baking sheets with baking paper.

4. Unwrap the dough and roll out between two sheets of baking paper. Stamp out circles with a 6-cm/2½-inch round cutter and put them on the prepared baking sheets, spaced well apart.

5. Bake in the preheated oven for 10–12 minutes, or until golden brown. Leave to cool on the baking sheets for a few minutes, then transfer to wire racks to cool completely.

6. When the cookies are cool, place the wire racks over a sheet of baking paper. Put the chocolate into a heatproof bowl set over a saucepan of gently simmering water and stir until melted. Remove from the heat and leave to cool slightly. Spoon the chocolate over the cookies, gently tap the wire racks to level the surface and leave to set. Lightly dust with cocoa before serving.

Traditional Shortbread

makes 8

ingredients

175 g/6 oz plain flour,
plus extra for dusting

pinch of salt

55 g/2 oz caster sugar, plus
extra for sprinkling

115 g/4 oz unsalted butter,
cut into small pieces

1. Preheat the oven to 150°C/300°F/Gas Mark 2. Line a baking sheet with baking paper.

2. Place the flour, salt and sugar in a large bowl and mix together. Add the butter and rub it into the dry ingredients with your fingertips. Continue to work the mixture until it forms a soft dough. Make sure you do not overwork the shortbread or it will be tough.

3. Roll out the dough on a lightly floured surface to form a 20-cm/8-inch circle. Transfer to the prepared baking sheet and pinch the edges to form a scalloped pattern. Using a knife, mark the dough into eight pieces and prick all over with a fork.

4. Bake in the preheated oven for 45–50 minutes, or until the shortbread is firm and just coloured. Leave to cool on the baking sheet for a few minutes, then sprinkle with sugar. Cut into portions and transfer to a wire rack to cool completely.

2

3

4

Thumbprint Cookies

makes 36

ingredients

115 g/4 oz unsalted butter,
softened
125 g/4½ oz caster sugar
1 large egg, separated
1 tsp vanilla extract
175 g/6 oz plain flour
pinch of salt
25 g/1 oz ground almonds
100 g/3½ oz raspberry jam

1. Preheat the oven to 180°C/350°F/Gas Mark 4.
Line two large baking sheets with baking paper.

2. Place the butter and 100 g/3½ oz of the sugar in a
large bowl and beat until light and fluffy. Add the egg
yolk and vanilla extract and beat well to combine.
Sift in the flour and salt and mix well.

3. Mix together the remaining sugar and the ground
almonds and spread out on a plate. Lightly whisk
the egg white in a separate bowl.

4. Roll walnut-sized pieces of the dough into
balls, then dip each ball into the egg white and
roll in the almond sugar. Place the balls on the
prepared baking sheets, spaced well apart, and
make a deep indentation in the centre of each
cookie with your thumb.

5. Bake in the preheated oven for 10 minutes.
Remove from the oven, press down again on
each indentation and fill it with jam. Bake for a
further 10–12 minutes, or until the cookies are
golden brown. Leave to cool on the baking sheets
for a few minutes, then transfer to wire racks to
cool completely.

top tip

For a delicious variation,
replace the raspberry jam
with lemon curd.

Black & White Cookies

makes 20

ingredients

115 g/4 oz unsalted butter,
softened, plus extra
for greasing
1 tsp vanilla extract
175 g/6 oz caster sugar
2 eggs, beaten
300 g/10½ oz plain flour
½ tsp baking powder
200 ml/7 fl oz milk

topping

225 g/8 oz icing sugar
125 ml/4 fl oz double cream
a few drops of vanilla extract
75 g/2¾ oz plain chocolate,
broken into pieces

1. Preheat the oven to 190°C/375°F/Gas Mark 5.
Lightly grease three baking sheets.

2. Place the butter, vanilla extract and caster sugar
in a large bowl. Beat the mixture with an electric
mixer until light and fluffy, then beat in the eggs
one at a time.

3. Sift the flour and baking powder into a separate
bowl, then gradually fold the flour mixture into
the creamed mixture, loosening with the milk as
you go until both are used up and the mixture is of
dropping consistency.

4. Drop heaped tablespoonfuls of the mixture onto
the prepared baking sheets, spaced well apart.

5. Bake in the preheated oven for 15 minutes, or
until the cookies are turning golden at the edges
and are light to the touch. Leave to cool on the
baking sheets for a few minutes, then transfer to
wire racks to cool completely.

6. Put the icing sugar in a bowl and mix in half the
cream and the vanilla extract. The consistency
should be thick but spreadable. Using a palette knife,
spread half of each cookie with the white icing.

7. Place the chocolate in a heatproof bowl over
a saucepan of gently simmering water and stir
until melted. Remove from the heat and stir in the
remaining cream. Spread the dark icing over the
uncoated cookie halves and leave to set.

2

4

6

Melting Moments

makes 32

ingredients

350 g/12 oz unsalted butter, softened

85 g/3 oz icing sugar

½ tsp vanilla extract

300 g/10½ oz plain flour

50 g/1¾ oz cornflour

1. Preheat the oven to 180°C/350°F/Gas Mark 4. Line two large baking sheets with baking paper.

2. Place the butter and icing sugar in a large bowl and beat together until light and fluffy, then beat in the vanilla extract. Sift in the flour and cornflour and mix thoroughly.

3. Spoon the mixture into a piping bag fitted with a large star nozzle. Pipe rosette shapes onto the prepared baking sheets, spaced well apart.

4. Bake in the preheated oven for 15–20 minutes, or until golden brown. Leave to cool completely on the baking sheets.

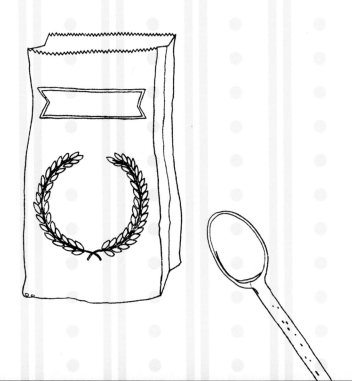

top tip
Make these cookies extra
special by dipping them
in melted chocolate.

Pistachio Biscotti

makes 30

ingredients

225 g/8 oz unsalted butter, softened

140 g/5 oz caster sugar

finely grated rind of 1 lemon

1 egg yolk, lightly beaten

2 tsp brandy

280 g/10 oz plain flour

pinch of salt

85 g/3 oz pistachio nuts

icing sugar, for dusting

1. Put the butter, caster sugar and lemon rind into a bowl and mix well with a wooden spoon, then beat in the egg yolk and brandy. Sift the flour and salt into the mixture and stir in the pistachio nuts until thoroughly combined.

2. Shape the mixture into a log and flatten slightly, then wrap in clingfilm and chill in the refrigerator for 30–60 minutes.

3. Preheat the oven to 190°C/375°F/Gas Mark 5. Line two baking sheets with baking paper.

4. Unwrap the log and cut it slightly on the diagonal into 5-mm/¼-inch slices with a sharp, serrated knife. Put them on the prepared baking sheets, spaced well apart.

5. Bake in the preheated oven for 10 minutes, or until golden brown. Leave to cool on the baking sheets for a few minutes, then transfer to wire racks to cool completely. Dust with icing sugar before serving.

1

2

4

Snickerdoodles

makes 40

ingredients

225 g/8 oz unsalted butter,
softened

140 g/5 oz caster sugar

2 large eggs, lightly beaten

1 tsp vanilla extract

400 g/14 oz plain flour

1 tsp bicarbonate of soda

½ tsp freshly grated nutmeg

pinch of salt

55 g/2 oz pecan nuts,
finely chopped

cinnamon coating

1 tbsp caster sugar

2 tbsp ground cinnamon

1. Put the butter and sugar into a bowl and mix well with a wooden spoon, then beat in the eggs and vanilla extract. Sift the flour, bicarbonate of soda, nutmeg and salt into the mixture, add the pecan nuts and stir until thoroughly combined.

2. Shape the dough into a ball, wrap in clingfilm and chill in the refrigerator for 30–60 minutes.

3. Preheat the oven to 190°C/375°F/Gas Mark 5. Line two or three baking sheets with baking paper.

4. To make the cinnamon coating, mix together the sugar and cinnamon in a shallow dish. Scoop up tablespoons of the cookie dough and roll into balls. Roll each ball in the cinnamon mixture to coat and place on the prepared baking sheets, spaced well apart.

5. Bake in the preheated oven for 10–12 minutes, until golden brown. Leave to cool on the baking sheets for a few minutes, then transfer to wire racks to cool completely.

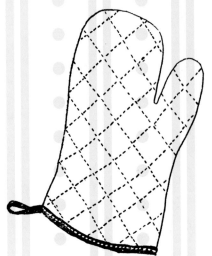

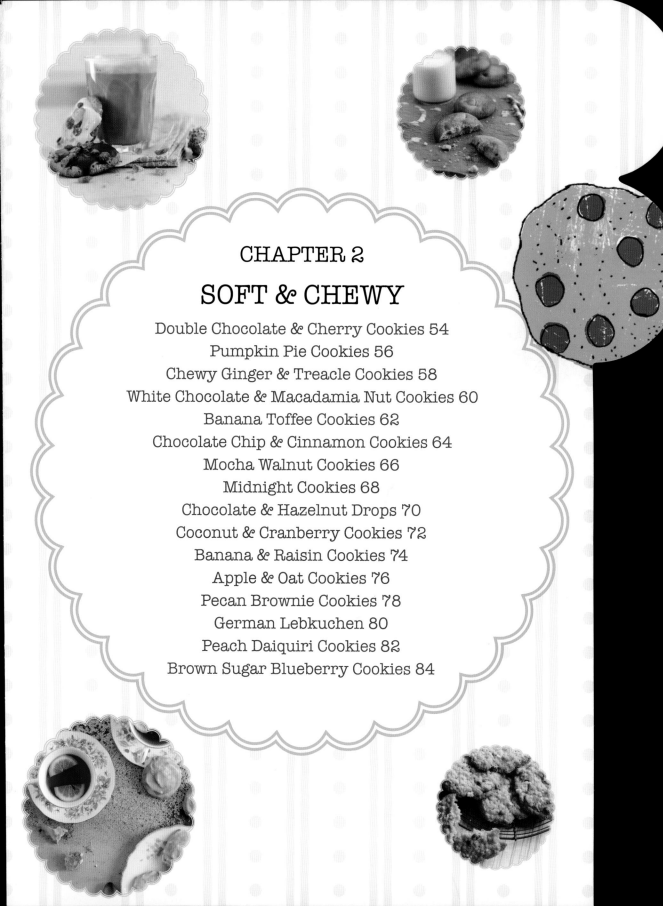

CHAPTER 2

SOFT & CHEWY

Double Chocolate & Cherry Cookies

makes 30

ingredients

225 g/8 oz unsalted butter,
softened

140 g/5 oz caster sugar

1 egg yolk, lightly beaten

2 tsp vanilla extract

250 g/9 oz plain flour

25 g/1 oz cocoa powder

pinch of salt

350 g/12 oz plain chocolate,
chopped

55 g/2 oz dried sour cherries

1. Preheat the oven to 190°C/375°F/Gas Mark 5.
Line two baking sheets with baking paper.

2. Put the butter and sugar into a bowl and mix well
with a wooden spoon, then beat in the egg yolk and
vanilla extract. Sift the flour, cocoa and salt into
the mixture, add the chopped chocolate and sour
cherries and stir until thoroughly combined.

3. Scoop up tablespoons of the mixture and shape
into balls. Put them on the prepared baking sheets,
spaced well apart, and flatten slightly.

4. Bake in the preheated oven for 12–15 minutes.
Leave to cool on the baking sheets for a few minutes,
then transfer to wire racks to cool completely.

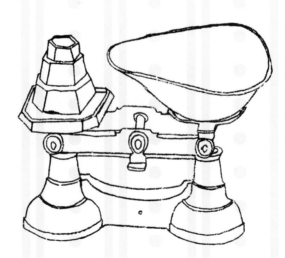

top tip
Use a plain chocolate with
a high percentage of cocoa
solids for this recipe.

Pumpkin Pie Cookies

makes 20

ingredients

115 g/4 oz unsalted butter,
softened

115 g/4 oz caster sugar

115 g/4 oz light muscovado
sugar

1 egg, lightly beaten

½ tsp vanilla extract

150 g/5½ oz canned
pumpkin purée

250 g/9 oz plain flour

¼ tsp salt

1½ tsp ground cinnamon

¼ tsp each ground ginger,
ground cloves and
freshly grated nutmeg

glaze

125 g/4½ oz icing sugar

1 tbsp maple syrup

1–2 tbsp warm water

1. Preheat the oven to 180°C/350°F/Gas Mark 4. Line three baking sheets with baking paper.

2. Place the butter and sugars in a large bowl and beat together until pale and fluffy. Gradually beat in the egg, then stir in the vanilla extract and pumpkin purée. Sift in the flour, salt and spices and stir until thoroughly combined.

3. Place 20 dessertspoonfuls of the mixture onto the prepared baking sheets and spread each out to a 6-cm/2½-inch circle with the back of a spoon.

4. Bake in the preheated oven for 15–20 minutes, or until golden and firm to the touch. Leave to cool on the baking sheets for a few minutes, then transfer to wire racks to cool completely.

5. To make the glaze, sift the icing sugar into a bowl. Add the maple syrup and 1 tablespoon of warm water and beat together until smooth. Add a little extra water, if needed, to give a fairly runny consistency. Spoon the glaze over the pumpkin cookies and leave to set.

2

3

5

Chewy Ginger & Treacle Cookies

makes 28

ingredients

115 g/4 oz unsalted butter,
plus extra for greasing

85 g/3 oz black treacle

350 g/12 oz self-raising flour

1 tsp bicarbonate of soda

2 tsp ground ginger

1 tsp ground cinnamon

175 g/6 oz light muscovado
sugar

1 large egg, beaten

2 tbsp demerara sugar

1. Preheat the oven to 160°C/325°F/Gas Mark 3. Lightly grease two or three large baking sheets.

2. Place the butter and black treacle in a small saucepan and heat gently until the butter has melted. Leave to cool for 10 minutes.

3. Sift the flour, bicarbonate of soda and spices into a large bowl. Stir in the muscovado sugar and make a well in the centre. Pour in the cooled butter mixture and the egg and mix thoroughly to form a crumbly dough. Use your hands to gather the dough together.

4. Shape the dough into 28 walnut-sized balls. Place on the prepared baking sheets, spaced well apart, and flatten each one slightly. Sprinkle over the demerara sugar.

5. Bake in the preheated oven for 10–12 minutes, or until just set and the surfaces are cracked. Leave to cool on the baking sheets for a few minutes, then transfer to wire racks to cool completely.

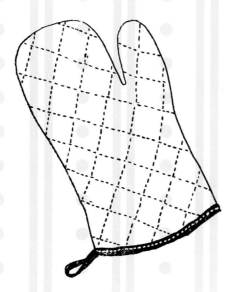

2

3

4

White Chocolate & Macadamia Nut Cookies

makes 16

ingredients

115 g/4 oz unsalted butter,
softened, plus extra
for greasing

115 g/4 oz soft light
brown sugar

1 tbsp golden syrup

175 g/6 oz self-raising flour

55 g/2 oz macadamia nuts,
roughly chopped

55 g/2 oz white chocolate,
cut into chunks

1. Preheat the oven to 180°C/350°F/Gas Mark 4. Lightly grease two large baking sheets.

2. Put the butter and sugar into a bowl and beat until pale and creamy, then beat in the golden syrup. Sift in the flour, add the nuts and mix to form a rough dough.

3. Shape the dough into 16 equal-sized balls and place on the prepared baking sheets, spaced well apart. Slightly flatten each ball and top with the chocolate chunks, pressing them lightly into the dough.

4. Bake in the preheated oven for 12–14 minutes, or until just set and pale golden. Leave to cool on the baking sheets for a few minutes, then transfer to wire racks to cool completely.

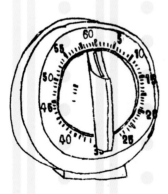

2

3

4

Banana Toffee Cookies

makes 16

ingredients

115 g/4 oz unsalted butter, softened

100 g/3 ½ oz light muscovado sugar

1 tbsp maple syrup

1 small banana, peeled and mashed (100 g/3½ oz peeled weight)

225 g/8 oz self-raising flour

55 g/2 oz hard toffees, roughly crushed

1. Preheat the oven to 180°C/350°F/Gas Mark 4. Line two large baking sheets with baking paper.

2. Place the butter, sugar and maple syrup in a large bowl and beat until pale and creamy. Stir in the mashed banana. Sift in the flour and mix to form a soft, slightly sticky dough. Stir in the crushed toffees.

3. Shape the dough into 16 walnut-sized balls. Place on the prepared baking sheets, spaced well apart, and flatten each one slightly.

4. Bake in the preheated oven for 11–12 minutes, or until pale golden. Leave to cool on the baking sheets for a few minutes, then transfer to wire racks to cool completely.

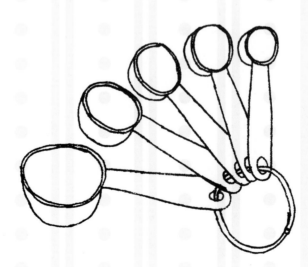

2   3   4

Chocolate Chip & Cinnamon Cookies

makes 30

ingredients

225 g/8 oz unsalted butter, softened

140 g/5 oz caster sugar

1 egg yolk, lightly beaten

2 tsp orange extract

280 g/10 g plain flour

pinch of salt

100 g/3½ oz plain chocolate chips

cinnamon coating

1½ tbsp caster sugar

1½ tbsp ground cinnamon

1. Preheat the oven to 190°C/375°F/Gas Mark 5. Line two baking sheets with baking paper.

2. Put the butter and sugar into a bowl and mix well with a wooden spoon, then beat in the egg yolk with orange extract. Sift the flour and salt into the mixture, add the chocolate chips and stir until thoroughly combined.

3. For the cinnamon coating, mix together the caster sugar and cinnamon in a shallow dish.

4. Scoop up tablespoons of the cookie dough and roll them into balls, then roll them in the cinnamon mixture to coat. Put them on the prepared baking sheets, spaced well apart.

5. Bake in the preheated oven for 12–15 minutes. Leave to cool on the baking sheets for a few minutes, then transfer to wire racks to cool completely.

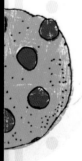

Mocha Walnut Cookies

makes 16

ingredients

115 g/4 oz unsalted butter, softened, plus extra for greasing

115 g/4 oz light muscovado sugar

85 g/3 oz caster sugar

1 tsp vanilla extract

1 tbsp instant coffee granules, dissolved in 1 tbsp hot water

1 egg

175 g/6 oz plain flour

½ tsp baking powder

¼ tsp bicarbonate of soda

55 g/2 oz milk chocolate chips

55 g/2 oz walnut halves, roughly chopped

1. Preheat the oven to 180°C/350°F/Gas Mark 4. Lightly grease two large baking sheets.

2. Place the butter and sugars in a large bowl and beat together until light and fluffy. Place the vanilla extract, coffee and egg in a separate bowl and whisk together. Gradually add the coffee mixture to the creamed mixture, beating until fluffy. Sift the flour, baking powder and bicarbonate of soda into the mixture and fold in carefully. Fold in the chocolate chips and walnuts.

3. Spoon heaped teaspoonfuls of the mixture onto the prepared baking sheets, spaced well apart.

4. Bake in the preheated oven for 10–15 minutes, or until crisp on the outside but soft inside. Leave to cool on the baking sheets for a few minutes, then transfer to wire racks to cool completely.

top tip

Try using plain or white chocolate chips instead of the milk chocolate chips.

Midnight Cookies

makes 25

ingredients

125 g/4½ oz unsalted butter, softened
175 g/6 oz caster sugar
1 egg, lightly beaten
½ tsp vanilla extract
125 g/4½ oz plain flour
35 g/1¼ oz cocoa powder
½ tsp bicarbonate of soda
melted plain chocolate, to serve (optional)

1. Preheat the oven to 180°C/350°F/Gas Mark 4. Line several large baking sheets with baking paper.

2. Place the butter and sugar in a large bowl and beat together until light and fluffy. Add the egg and vanilla extract and mix until smooth. Sift in the flour, cocoa and bicarbonate of soda and beat until well mixed.

3. With dampened hands, roll walnut-sized pieces of the dough into smooth balls. Place on the prepared baking sheets, spaced well apart.

4. Bake in the preheated oven for 10–12 minutes, or until set. Leave to cool on the baking sheets for a few minutes, then transfer to wire racks to cool completely. If wished, serve with a small bowl of melted plain chocolate for dipping.

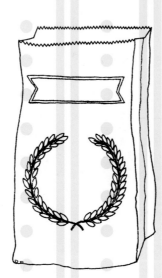

2

3

3

Chocolate & Hazelnut Drops

makes 30

ingredients

225 g/8 oz unsalted butter, softened

140 g/5 oz caster sugar

1 egg yolk, lightly beaten

2 tsp vanilla extract

225 g/8 oz plain flour

55 g/2 oz cocoa powder

pinch of salt

55 g/2 oz ground hazelnuts

55 g/2 oz plain chocolate chips

4 tbsp chocolate hazelnut spread

1. Preheat the oven to 190°C/375°F/Gas Mark 5. Line two baking sheets with baking paper.

2. Put the butter and sugar into a bowl and mix well with a wooden spoon, then beat in the egg yolk and vanilla extract. Sift the flour, cocoa and salt into the mixture, then add the ground hazelnuts and chocolate chips and stir until thoroughly combined.

3. Scoop up tablespoonfuls of the mixture and shape into balls with your hands, then put them on the prepared baking sheets, spaced well apart. Use the dampened handle of a wooden spoon to make a hollow in the centre of each cookie.

4. Bake in the preheated oven for 12–15 minutes. Leave to cool on the baking sheets for a few minutes, then transfer to wire racks to cool completely. When the cookies are cold, fill the hollows with the chocolate hazelnut spread.

top tip

For a change, fill with peanut butter instead of the chocolate hazelnut spread.

Coconut & Cranberry Cookies

makes 30

ingredients

225 g/8 oz unsalted butter,
softened

140 g/5 oz caster sugar

1 egg yolk

2 tsp vanilla extract

280 g/10 oz plain flour

pinch of salt

40 g/1½ oz desiccated coconut

60 g/2¼ oz dried cranberries

1. Preheat the oven to 190°C/375°F/Gas Mark 5. Line several baking sheets with baking paper.

2. Put the butter and sugar into a bowl and beat together until pale and creamy, then beat in the egg yolk and vanilla extract. Sift the flour and salt into the mixture, add the coconut and cranberries and stir until thoroughly combined.

3. Scoop up tablespoonfuls of the dough and place in mounds on the prepared baking sheets, spaced well apart.

4. Bake in the preheated oven for 12–15 minutes, or until golden brown. Leave to cool on the baking sheets for a few minutes, then transfer to wire racks to cool completely.

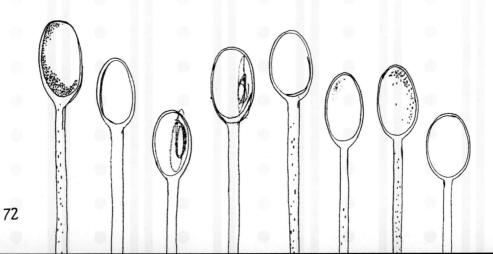

2

2

3

Banana & Raisin Cookies

makes 30

ingredients

25 g/1 oz raisins

125 ml/4 fl oz orange juice or rum

225 g/8 oz unsalted butter, softened

140 g/5 oz caster sugar

1 egg yolk, lightly beaten

280 g/10 oz plain flour

pinch of salt

85 g/3 oz dried bananas, finely chopped

1. Put the raisins into a bowl, pour in the orange juice and leave to soak for 30 minutes. Drain the raisins, reserving any remaining orange juice.

2. Preheat the oven to 190°C/375°F/Gas Mark 5. Line two baking sheets with baking paper.

3. Put the butter and sugar into a bowl and mix well with a wooden spoon, then beat in the egg yolk and 2 teaspoons of the reserved orange juice. Sift the flour and salt into the mixture, add the raisins and dried bananas and stir until thoroughly combined.

4. Put tablespoonfuls of the mixture into heaps on the prepared baking sheets, spaced well apart, then flatten them gently.

5. Bake in the preheated oven for 12–15 minutes, until golden. Leave to cool on the baking sheets for a few minutes, then transfer to wire racks to cool completely.

top tip
For a tropical taste, replace the raisins with finely chopped dried mango.

Apple & Oat Cookies

makes 26

ingredients

2 large apples, peeled and cored (200 g/7 oz unpeeled weight)

1 tsp lemon juice

225 g/8 oz unsalted butter, softened, plus extra for greasing

100 g/3½ oz soft light brown sugar

100 g/3½ oz caster sugar

1 egg, beaten

225 g/8 oz self-raising flour

150 g/5½ oz rolled oats

85 g/3 oz raisins

1. Preheat the oven to 180°C/350°F/Gas Mark 4. Grease three large baking sheets. Finely dice the apples and toss in the lemon juice.

2. Place the butter and sugars in a bowl and beat together until creamy. Gradually beat in the egg. Sift in the flour and add the oats, raisins and apples. Mix until thoroughly combined.

3. Place dessertspoonfuls of the mixture on the prepared baking sheets, spaced well apart.

4. Bake in the preheated oven for 12–15 minutes, or until golden around the edges. Leave to cool on the baking sheets for a few minutes, then transfer to wire racks to cool completely.

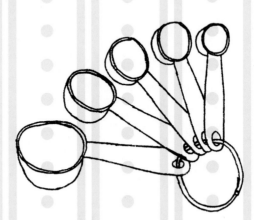

1

2

4

Pecan Brownie Cookies

makes 18

ingredients

150 g/5½ oz plain chocolate, broken into pieces

85 g/3 oz unsalted butter, softened

175 g/6 oz light muscovado sugar

2 eggs, lightly beaten

1 tsp vanilla extract

175 g/6 oz plain flour

½ tsp baking powder

85 g/3 oz pecan nuts, chopped

1. Preheat the oven to 190°C/375°F/Gas Mark 5. Line two large baking sheets with baking paper.

2. Place the chocolate in a heatproof bowl set over a saucepan of gently simmering water and stir until melted. Remove from the heat and leave to cool for 10 minutes.

3. Place the butter and sugar in a large bowl and beat together until pale and creamy. Gradually beat in the eggs, then stir in the vanilla extract and cooled melted chocolate.

4. Sift in the flour and baking powder and add 55 g/2 oz of the chopped pecans. Stir until thoroughly combined.

5. Drop 18 heaped dessertspoonfuls of the mixture onto the prepared baking sheets, spaced well apart. Flatten each one slightly with the back of the spoon and top with the remaining chopped pecans.

6. Bake for 18 minutes, or until just firm to the touch. Leave to cool on the baking sheets for a few minutes, then transfer to wire racks to cool completely.

top tip

If you like, drizzle the cooled cookies with melted white chocolate.

German Lebkuchen

makes 60

ingredients

3 eggs

200 g/7 oz caster sugar

55 g/2 oz plain flour

2 tsp cocoa powder

1 tsp ground cinnamon

½ tsp ground cardamom

¼ tsp ground cloves

¼ tsp ground nutmeg

175 g/6 oz ground almonds

55 g/2 oz mixed peel,
finely chopped

topping

115 g/4 oz plain chocolate,
broken into pieces

115 g/4 oz white chocolate,
broken into pieces

sugar crystals, to decorate

1. Preheat the oven to 180°C/350°F/Gas Mark 4.
Line several large baking sheets with baking paper.

2. Place the eggs and sugar in a heatproof bowl set
over a saucepan of gently simmering water and,
using an electric mixer, whisk until thick and foamy.
Remove the bowl from the pan and continue to
whisk for 2 minutes.

3. Sift the flour, cocoa, cinnamon, cardamom, cloves
and nutmeg into the bowl and stir in with the
ground almonds and mixed peel.

4. Drop heaped teaspoonfuls of the mixture onto
the prepared baking sheets, spreading them gently
into smooth mounds.

5. Bake in the preheated oven for 15–20 minutes,
or until light brown and slightly soft to the touch.
Leave to cool on the baking sheets for a few minutes,
then transfer to wire racks to cool completely.

6. Place the plain and white chocolate in separate
heatproof bowls each set over a pan of gently
simmering water and stir until melted. Remove
from the heat and leave to cool slightly.

7. Spoon the melted plain chocolate over half the
cookies and the melted white chocolate over the rest
and place on a wire rack set over a sheet of baking
paper. Sprinkle with sugar crystals and leave to set.

2

5

7

Peach Daiquiri Cookies

makes 30

ingredients

225 g/8 oz unsalted butter, softened

140 g/5 oz caster sugar

finely grated rind of 1 lime

1 egg yolk, lightly beaten

2 tsp white rum

280 g/10 oz plain flour

pinch of salt

100 g/3½ oz ready-to-eat dried peach, chopped

icing

140 g/5 oz icing sugar

1–2 tbsp white rum

1. Preheat the oven to 190°C/375°F/Gas Mark 5. Line two baking sheets with baking paper.

2. Put the butter, caster sugar and lime rind into a bowl and mix well with a wooden spoon, then beat in the egg yolk and rum. Sift the flour and salt into the mixture, add the peach and stir until thoroughly combined.

3. Scoop up tablespoonfuls of the dough and put them on the prepared baking sheets, spaced well apart, then flatten gently.

4. Bake in the preheated oven for 10–15 minutes, until light golden brown. Leave to cool on the baking sheets for a few minutes, then transfer to wire racks to cool completely.

5. Sift the icing sugar into a bowl and stir in enough of the rum to give the mixture the consistency of thick cream. Leave the cookies on the racks and drizzle the icing over them with a teaspoon. Leave to set.

top tip

To add a fruity flavour to the icing, use peach juice instead of the rum.

Soft & Chewy
CHAPTER 2

Brown Sugar Blueberry Cookies

makes 18

ingredients

115 g/4 oz unsalted butter, softened

150 g/5½ oz light muscovado sugar

1 egg, lightly beaten

1 tsp vanilla extract

225 g/8 oz plain flour

pinch of salt

¾ tsp baking powder

1 tsp ground cinnamon

2 tbsp milk

125 g/4½ oz fresh blueberries

1. Preheat the oven to 190°C/375°F/Gas Mark 5. Line three baking sheets with baking paper.

2. Place the butter and sugar in a large bowl and, using an electric mixer, beat together until smooth and creamy. Gradually beat in the egg and the vanilla extract.

3. Sift in the flour, salt, baking powder and cinnamon and add the milk. Mix thoroughly with a wooden spoon or spatula to make a soft, sticky dough. Fold in the blueberries.

4. Place 18 heaped dessertspoonfuls of the mixture onto the prepared baking sheets, spaced well apart.

5. Bake in the preheated oven for 11–12 minutes, or until puffy and pale golden. Leave to cool on the baking sheets for a few minutes, then transfer to wire racks to cool completely.

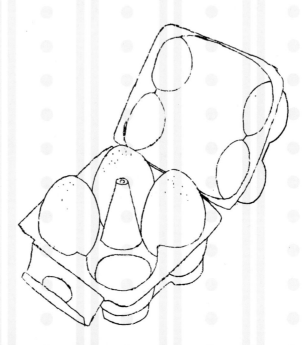

2

3

5

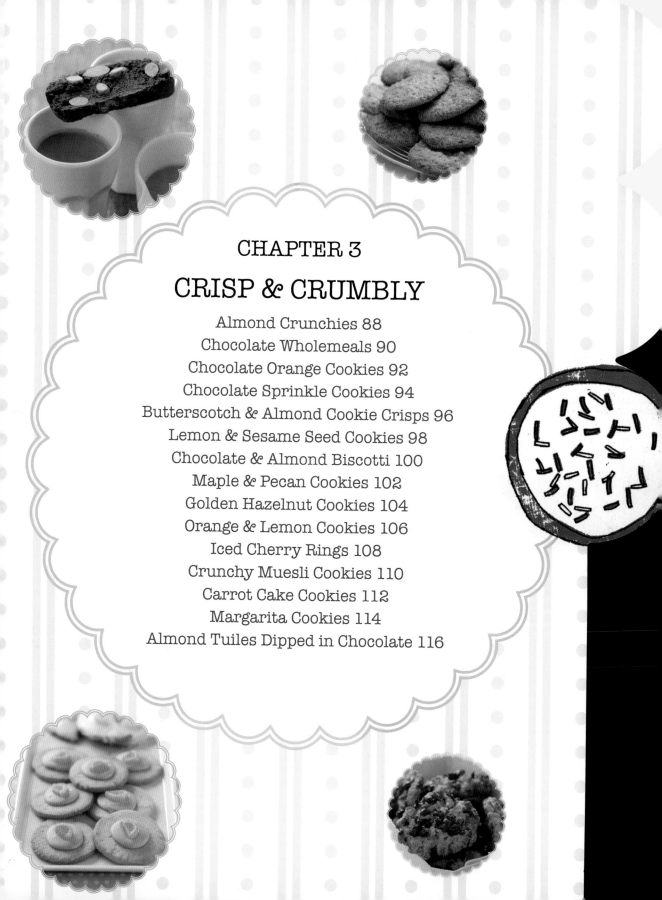

CHAPTER 3
CRISP & CRUMBLY

Almond Crunchies

makes 50

ingredients

225 g/8 oz unsalted butter, softened

140 g/5 oz caster sugar

1 egg yolk, lightly beaten

½ tsp almond extract

225 g/8 oz plain flour

pinch of salt

225 g/8 oz blanched almonds, chopped

1. Put the butter and sugar into a bowl and mix well with a wooden spoon, then beat in the egg yolk and almond extract. Sift the flour and salt into the mixture, add the almonds and stir until thoroughly combined.

2. Halve the dough and shape into two balls, then wrap in clingfilm and chill in the refrigerator for 30–60 minutes.

3. Preheat the oven to 190°C/375°F/Gas Mark 5. Line two or three baking sheets with baking paper.

4. Unwrap the dough, shape into 50 small balls and flatten them slightly between the palms of your hands. Put on the prepared baking sheets, spaced well apart.

5. Bake in the preheated oven for 15–20 minutes, until golden brown. Leave to cool on the baking sheets for a few minutes, then transfer to wire racks to cool completely.

top tip

These cookies are an
excellent accompaniment to
a creamy dessert.

89

Chocolate Wholemeals

makes 20

ingredients

75 g/2¾ oz unsalted butter
125 g/4½ oz demerara sugar
1 egg
1 tbsp wheatgerm
150 g/5½ oz wholemeal
self-raising flour
70 g/2½ oz white
self-raising flour
125 g/4½ oz plain chocolate,
broken into pieces

1. Preheat the oven to 180°C/350°F/Gas Mark 4. Line two or three baking sheets with baking paper.

2. Place the butter and sugar in a large bowl and beat together until light and fluffy. Add the egg and beat well. Stir in the wheatgerm and flours, then bring the mixture together with your hands.

3. Roll rounded teaspoonfuls of the mixture into balls. Place them on the prepared baking sheets, spaced well apart, then flatten slightly.

4. Bake in the preheated oven for 15–20 minutes, or until golden brown. Leave to cool on the baking sheets for a few minutes, then transfer to wire racks to cool completely.

5. Place the chocolate in a heatproof bowl set over a saucepan of gently simmering water and stir until melted. Dip each cookie in the chocolate to cover the flat side and a little way around the edges. Allow any excess chocolate to drip back into the bowl. Place the cookies on a sheet of baking paper in a cool place and leave to set.

Crisp & Crumbly
CHAPTER 3

Chocolate Orange Cookies

makes 30

ingredients

90 g/3¼ oz unsalted butter, softened

60 g/2¼ oz caster sugar

1 egg

1 tbsp milk

280 g/10 oz plain flour, plus extra for dusting

2 tbsp cocoa powder

topping

175 g/6 oz icing sugar

2–3 tbsp orange juice

100 g/3½ oz plain chocolate, broken into pieces

1. Preheat the oven to 180°C/350°F/Gas Mark 4. Line two large baking sheets with baking paper.

2. Place the butter and caster sugar in a large bowl and beat together until light and fluffy. Beat in the egg and milk until thoroughly combined. Sift the flour and cocoa into the bowl and gradually mix together to form a soft dough.

3. Roll out the dough on a lightly floured surface until about 5 mm/¼ inch thick. Cut out circles with a 5-cm/2-inch fluted round cutter and transfer to the prepared baking sheets.

4. Bake in the preheated oven for 10–12 minutes, or until golden. Leave to cool on the baking sheets for a few minutes, then transfer to wire racks to cool completely and become crisp.

5. Sift the icing sugar into a bowl and stir in enough of the orange juice to form a thin icing that will coat the back of the spoon. Place a spoonful of icing in the centre of each cookie and leave to set.

6. Place the chocolate in a heatproof bowl set over a saucepan of gently simmering water and heat until melted. Leave to cool slightly, then spoon into a paper piping bag and snip off the end. Drizzle the melted chocolate over the cookies and leave to set before serving.

Chocolate Sprinkle Cookies

makes 30

ingredients

225 g/8 oz unsalted butter,
softened

140 g/5 oz caster sugar

1 egg yolk, lightly beaten

2 tsp vanilla extract

225 g/8 oz plain flour,
plus extra for dusting

55 g/2 oz cocoa powder

pinch of salt

topping

200 g/7 oz white chocolate,
broken into pieces

85 g/3 oz chocolate sprinkles

1. Put the butter and sugar into a bowl and mix well with a wooden spoon, then beat in the egg yolk and vanilla extract. Sift the flour, cocoa and salt into the mixture and stir until thoroughly combined.

2. Halve the dough and shape into two balls, then wrap in clingfilm and chill in the refrigerator for 30–60 minutes.

3. Preheat the oven to 190°C/375°F/Gas Mark 5. Line two baking sheets with baking paper.

4. Unwrap the dough and roll out between two sheets of baking paper to about 5 mm/¼ inch thick. Stamp out 30 cookies with a 6–7-cm/2½ –2¾-inch fluted round cutter. Put them on the prepared baking sheets, spaced well apart.

5. Bake in the preheated oven for 10–12 minutes. Leave to cool on the baking sheets for a few minutes, then transfer to wire racks to cool completely.

6. Put the chocolate into a heatproof bowl set over a pan of gently simmering water and stir until melted. Remove from the heat. Spread the melted chocolate over the cookies and leave to cool slightly, then scatter over the chocolate sprinkles. Leave to set.

top tip

Instead of using sprinkles, decorate with a swirl of melted plain chocolate.

Butterscotch & Almond
Cookie Crisps

makes 18

ingredients

2 egg whites

115 g/4 oz light muscovado
sugar

½ tsp vanilla extract

50 g/1¾ oz unsalted butter,
melted and cooled

55 g/2 oz plain flour

3 tbsp flaked almonds

1. Preheat the oven to 180°C/350°F/Gas Mark 4.
Line three baking sheets with baking paper.

2. Place the egg whites in a large bowl and, using a
balloon whisk, beat until frothy. Add the sugar and
vanilla extract and whisk for 2–3 minutes. Whisk
in the melted butter, then sift in the flour and mix
thoroughly to make a smooth, thick batter.

3. Drop dessertspoonfuls of the mixture onto the
prepared baking sheets, spaced well apart. Using the
back of the spoon, spread each spoonful of mixture
to form a 9-cm/3½-inch circle. Sprinkle over the
flaked almonds.

4. Bake in the preheated oven for 8–10 minutes,
or until the cookies are deep golden brown around
the edges. Leave to cool on the baking sheets
for a few minutes, then transfer to wire racks
to cool completely.

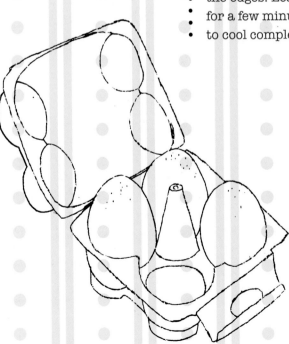

Lemon & Sesame Seed Cookies

makes 30

ingredients

2 tbsp sesame seeds

225 g/8 oz unsalted butter, softened

140 g/5 oz caster sugar

1 tbsp finely grated lemon rind

1 egg yolk, lightly beaten

280 g/10 oz plain flour

pinch of salt

icing

115 g/4 oz icing sugar

a few drops of lemon extract

1 tbsp hot water

1. Dry-fry the sesame seeds in a heavy-based frying pan over a low heat, stirring frequently, for 2–3 minutes, or until they give off their aroma. Tip out of the pan and leave to cool.

2. Place the butter, caster sugar, lemon rind and toasted seeds in a large bowl and beat together until light and fluffy, then beat in the egg yolk. Sift the flour and salt into the mixture and stir until combined.

3. Halve the dough and shape it into two balls, then wrap in clingfilm and chill in the refrigerator for 30–60 minutes.

4. Preheat the oven to 190°C/375°F/Gas Mark 5. Line two large baking sheets with baking paper.

5. Unwrap the dough and roll out between two sheets of baking paper. Cut out circles with a 6-cm/2½-inch plain round cutter and place them on the prepared baking sheets, spaced well apart.

6. Bake in the preheated oven for 10–12 minutes, or until light golden brown. Leave to cool on the baking sheets for a few minutes, then transfer to wire racks to cool completely.

7. To make the icing, sift the icing sugar into a bowl, add the lemon extract and gradually stir in the water to form a smooth icing with the consistency of thick cream. Leave the cooled cookies on the racks and spread the icing over them. Leave to set.

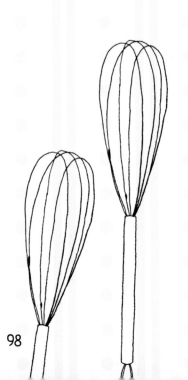

Chocolate & Almond Biscotti

makes 24

ingredients

unsalted butter, for greasing

150 g/5½ oz blanched almonds

150 g/5½ oz plain chocolate, broken into pieces

250 g/9 oz plain flour, plus extra for dusting

1 tsp baking powder

150 g/5½ oz caster sugar

2 large eggs, lightly beaten

1 tsp vanilla extract

1. Preheat the oven to 160°C/325°F/Gas Mark 3. Lightly grease a large baking sheet. Spread out the almonds on a separate baking sheet and bake in the preheated oven for 5–10 minutes, or until toasted. Leave to cool.

2. Place the chocolate in a heatproof bowl set over a saucepan of gently simmering water and stir until melted. Remove from the heat and leave to cool.

3. Sift the flour and baking powder into a large bowl. Add the sugar, toasted almonds, melted chocolate, eggs and vanilla extract and mix together to form a soft dough.

4. Turn out the dough onto a lightly floured surface and, with floured hands, knead for 2–3 minutes, or until smooth. Divide the dough in half and shape each portion into a log shape measuring about 5 cm/2 inches in diameter. Place the logs on the prepared baking sheet and flatten until each is about 2.5 cm/1 inch thick.

5. Bake in the preheated oven for 20–30 minutes, or until firm to the touch. Leave to cool on the baking sheet for 15 minutes. Meanwhile, reduce the oven temperature to 150°C/300°F/Gas Mark 2.

6. Using a serrated knife, cut the baked dough into 1 cm/½ inch thick slices and place on ungreased baking sheets. Bake in the oven for 10 minutes. Turn and bake for a further 10–15 minutes, until crisp. Transfer to wire racks to cool completely.

Maple & Pecan Cookies

makes 18

ingredients

85 g/3 oz pecan nut halves

115 g/4 oz unsalted butter, softened, plus extra for greasing

2 tbsp maple syrup

85 g/3 oz light muscovado sugar

1 large egg yolk, lightly beaten

115 g/4 oz self-raising flour

1. Preheat the oven to 190°C/375°F/Gas Mark 5. Lightly grease two baking sheets. Reserve 18 pecan halves and roughly chop the rest.

2. Place the butter, maple syrup and sugar in a bowl and beat together with a wooden spoon until light and fluffy. Beat in the egg yolk. Sift in the flour and add the chopped pecan nuts. Mix to form a stiff dough.

3. Place 18 spoonfuls of the mixture on the prepared baking sheets, spaced well apart. Top each with one of the reserved pecan nut halves, pressing down gently.

4. Bake in the preheated oven for 10–12 minutes, until light golden brown. Leave to cool on the baking sheets for a few minutes, then transfer to wire racks to cool completely.

102

top tip

For an indulgent variation, drizzle melted chocolate over the cooled cookies.

Crisp & Crumbly
CHAPTER 3

Golden Hazelnut Cookies

makes 30

ingredients

225 g/8 oz unsalted butter,
softened

140 g/5 oz golden caster sugar

1 egg yolk, lightly beaten

225 g/8 oz plain flour

pinch of salt

55 g/2 oz ground hazelnuts

topping

225 g/8 oz plain chocolate,
broken into pieces

30 hazelnuts

1. Put the butter and sugar into a bowl and mix well with a wooden spoon, then beat in the egg yolk. Sift the flour and salt into the mixture, add the ground hazelnuts and stir until thoroughly combined.

2. Halve the dough and shape into two balls, then wrap in clingfilm and chill in the refrigerator for 30–60 minutes.

3. Preheat the oven to 190°C/375°F/Gas Mark 5. Line two baking sheets with baking paper.

4. Unwrap the dough and roll out between two sheets of baking paper. Stamp out circles with a 6-cm/2½-inch plain round cutter and put them on the prepared baking sheets, spaced well apart.

5. Bake in the preheated oven for 10–12 minutes, until golden brown. Leave to cool on the baking sheets for a few minutes, then transfer to wire racks to cool completely.

6. When the cookies are cool, place the wire racks over a sheet of baking paper. Put the chocolate into a heatproof bowl set over a pan of gently simmering water and stir until melted. Remove the bowl from the heat and leave to cool slightly, then spoon the chocolate over the cookies. Gently tap the wire racks to level the surface, add a hazelnut to the centre of each cookie and leave to set.

top tip

For a topping with a twist, use melted white chocolate and chopped hazelnuts.

105

Orange & Lemon Cookies

makes 30

ingredients

225 g/8 oz unsalted butter,
softened

140 g/5 oz caster sugar

1 egg yolk, lightly beaten

280 g/10 oz plain flour

pinch of salt

finely grated rind of 1 orange

finely grated rind of 1 lemon

topping

1 tbsp lightly beaten egg white

1 tbsp lemon juice

115 g/4 oz icing sugar

yellow food colouring

orange food colouring

15 lemon jelly slices

15 orange jelly slices

1. Put the butter and caster sugar into a bowl and mix well with a wooden spoon, then beat in the egg yolk. Sift the flour and salt into the mixture and stir until thoroughly combined.

2. Halve the dough and gently knead the orange rind into one half and the lemon rind into the other. Shape into two balls, wrap in clingfilm and chill in the refrigerator for 30–60 minutes.

3. Preheat the oven to 190°C/375°F/Gas Mark 5. Line two baking sheets with baking paper.

4. Unwrap the orange-flavoured dough and roll out between two sheets of baking paper. Stamp out 15 circles with a 6-cm/2½-inch plain round cutter and put them on one of the prepared baking sheets, spaced well apart. Repeat with the lemon-flavoured dough, but stamp out crescents.

5. Bake in the preheated oven for 10–15 minutes, until golden brown. Leave to cool on the baking sheets for a few minutes, then transfer to wire racks to cool completely.

6. Mix together the egg white and lemon juice. Gradually beat in the icing sugar with a wooden spoon until smooth. Spoon half the icing into a separate bowl. Stir yellow food colouring into one bowl and orange food colouring into the other. Leave the cookies on the wire racks. Spread the orange icing over the orange-flavoured cookies and the yellow icing over the lemon-flavoured cookies. Decorate with the jelly slices and leave to set.

Iced Cherry Rings

makes 18

ingredients

115 g/4 oz unsalted butter,
plus extra for greasing
85 g/3 oz caster sugar
1 egg yolk
finely grated rind of ½ lemon
200 g/7 oz plain flour, plus
extra for dusting
55 g/2 oz glacé cherries,
finely chopped

icing

85 g/3 oz icing sugar
1½ tbsp lemon juice

1. Preheat the oven to 200°C/400°F/Gas Mark 6.
Lightly grease two large baking sheets.

2. Place the butter and caster sugar in a large bowl
and beat together until light and fluffy. Beat in the
egg yolk and lemon rind. Sift in the flour and stir,
then fold in the glacé cherries and mix to form a
soft dough.

3. Roll out the dough on a lightly floured surface to
5 mm/¼ inch thick. Stamp out 8-cm/3¼-inch circles
with a plain round cutter, then stamp out the centre
of each with a 2.5-cm/1-inch plain round cutter.
Place the rings on the prepared baking sheets.
Re-roll any trimmings and cut out more cookies.

4. Bake in the preheated oven for 12–15 minutes,
or until golden. Leave to cool on the baking sheets
for a few minutes, then transfer to wire racks to
cool completely.

5. To make the icing, mix the icing sugar and lemon
juice until smooth. Drizzle the icing over the cookies
and leave to set.

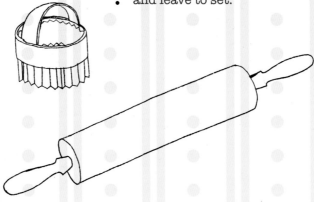

top tip

Try replacing the cherries with chopped mixed peel for a fruity change.

Crunchy Muesli Cookies

makes 24

ingredients

115 g/4 oz unsalted butter, softened, plus extra for greasing

85 g/3 oz demerara sugar

1 tbsp honey

115 g/4 oz self-raising flour

pinch of salt

60 g/2¼ oz ready-to-eat dried apricots, chopped

50 g/1¾ oz dried figs, chopped

115 g/4 oz porridge oats

1 tsp milk, if needed

40 g/1½ oz dried cranberries or sultanas

40 g/1½ oz walnut halves, chopped

1. Preheat the oven to 160°C/325°F/Gas Mark 3. Grease two large baking sheets.

2. Place the butter, sugar and honey in a saucepan and heat over a low heat until melted. Mix to combine. Sift the flour and salt into a large bowl and stir in the apricots, figs and oats. Pour in the butter and sugar mixture and mix to form a dough. If it is too stiff, add a little milk.

3. Divide the dough into 24 pieces and roll each piece into a ball. Place the balls on the prepared baking sheets, spaced well apart, and press flat to a diameter of 6 cm/2½ inches. Mix together the cranberries and walnuts and press into the cookies.

4. Bake in the preheated oven for 15 minutes. Leave to cool completely on the baking sheets.

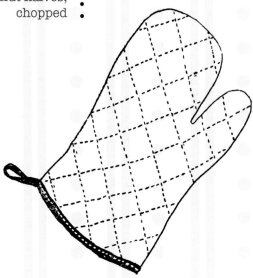

top tip

Use your favourite combo of dried fruits and nuts in this versatile recipe.

Crisp & Crumbly
CHAPTER 3

Carrot Cake Cookies

makes 30

ingredients

115 g/4 oz unsalted butter, softened

85 g/3 oz caster sugar

75 g/2¾ oz soft light brown sugar

1 large egg

½ tsp vanilla extract

150 g/5½ oz plain flour

½ tsp bicarbonate of soda

½ tsp ground cinnamon

85 g/3 oz carrots, finely grated

25 g/1 oz walnut halves, chopped

25 g/1 oz desiccated coconut

1. Preheat the oven to 190°C/375°F/Gas Mark 5. Line several large baking sheets with baking paper.

2. Place the butter and sugars in a large bowl and whisk together until pale and creamy. Whisk the egg and vanilla extract into the mixture until smooth. Sift in the flour, bicarbonate of soda and cinnamon, then beat together until well combined. Add the grated carrots, chopped walnuts and coconut to the mixture and mix together well.

3. Drop heaped teaspoonfuls of the mixture onto the prepared baking sheets, spaced well apart.

4. Bake in the preheated oven for 8-10 minutes, or until lightly golden brown around the edges. Leave to cool on the baking sheets for a few minutes, then transfer to wire racks to cool completely.

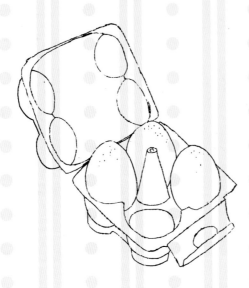

top tip

Make these cookies even more special by topping with cream cheese frosting.

Margarita Cookies

makes 30

ingredients

225 g/8 oz unsalted butter, softened

140 g/5 oz caster sugar

finely grated rind of 1 lime

1 egg yolk, lightly beaten

1 tsp orange extract

280 g/10 oz plain flour

pinch of salt

icing

140 g/5 oz icing sugar

1-2 tbsp white tequila

1. Preheat the oven to 190°C/375°F/Gas Mark 5. Line two baking sheets with baking paper.

2. Put the butter, caster sugar and lime rind into a bowl and mix well with a wooden spoon, then beat in the egg yolk and orange extract. Sift the flour and salt into the mixture and stir until thoroughly combined.

3. Scoop up tablespoonfuls of the dough and put them on the prepared baking sheets, spaced well apart, then flatten gently.

4. Bake in the preheated oven for 10-15 minutes, until light golden brown. Leave to cool on the baking sheets for a few minutes, then transfer to wire racks to cool completely.

5. Sift the icing sugar into a bowl and stir in enough of the tequila to give the mixture the consistency of thick cream. Leave the cookies on the wire racks and drizzle the icing over them with a teaspoon. Leave to set.

top tip

For Virgin Margarita Cookies, use lime juice in place of the tequila.

Almond Tuiles Dipped in Chocolate

makes 24

ingredients

1 tsp groundnut oil

85 g/3 oz unsalted butter, softened

70 g/2½ oz caster sugar

50 g/1¾ oz plain flour

pinch of salt

70 g/2½ oz flaked almonds

150 g/5½ oz plain chocolate, broken into pieces

1. Preheat the oven to 200°C/400°F/Gas Mark 6. Brush two large baking sheets with the oil.

2. Place the butter and sugar in a large bowl and beat together until light and fluffy. Sift in the flour and salt and fold into the mixture, then add the flaked almonds and mix together.

3. Drop teaspoonfuls of the mixture onto the prepared baking sheets, spaced well apart, and spread into flat ovals with the back of a spoon.

4. Bake, one baking sheet at a time, in the preheated oven for 5 minutes, or until golden. While the cookies are still warm, lift each one in turn and drape over a wooden rolling pin to make a curved shape. Leave to harden for 1 minute, then transfer to a wire rack to cool completely.

5. Place the chocolate in a heatproof bowl set over a saucepan of gently simmering water and stir until melted. Remove from the heat and leave to cool slightly. Dip one end of each of the tuiles into the melted chocolate, transfer to a sheet of baking paper or a wire rack and leave to set.

2 4 5

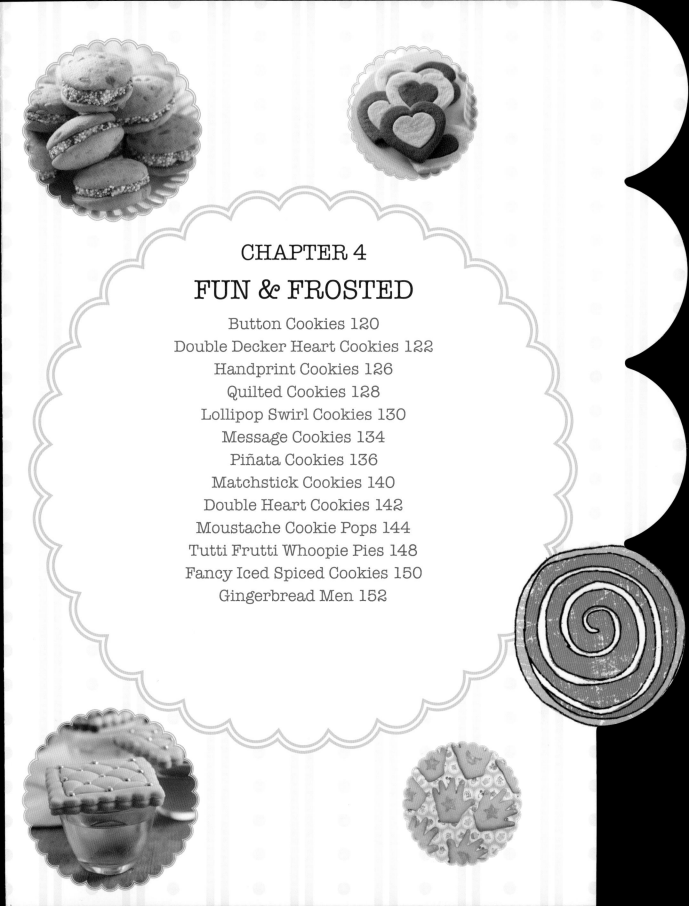

CHAPTER 4
FUN & FROSTED

Button Cookies

makes 26

ingredients

200 g/7 oz unsalted butter, softened

150 g/5½ oz caster sugar

1 large egg

2 tsp vanilla extract

400 g/14 oz plain flour

food colouring pastes in 3 different colours of your choice

1. Line two baking sheets with baking paper.

2. In a large bowl, cream the butter and sugar with an electric mixer until just coming together. Add the egg and vanilla extract and briefly whisk together.

3. Add the flour and use a wooden spoon to mix everything together to make a rough dough. Gather into a ball with your hands, then divide into three equal-sized portions. Knead a different food colouring into each portion of dough. Wrap each portion of dough in clingfilm and chill in the refrigerator for at least 10 minutes.

4. Unwrap the dough and roll out each portion between two large sheets of baking paper, turning the dough occasionally until it is an even thickness of about 5 mm/¼ inch. Using an 8-cm/3¼-inch plain round cutter, stamp out about 26 cookies in total, re-rolling each dough as necessary.

5. Transfer the cookies to the prepared baking sheets. Lightly press a 5-cm/2-inch plain round cutter into the centre of each cookie to make an indentation (don't cut all the way through), then use the tip of a plain piping nozzle to make four button holes in the centre of each. Chill in the refrigerator for 10 minutes. Meanwhile, preheat the oven to 180°C/350°F/Gas Mark 4.

6. Bake the cookies in the preheated oven for 15–18 minutes, or until just turning golden at the edges. Leave to cool on the baking sheets for a few minutes, then transfer to wire racks to cool completely.

3 4 5

Double Decker
Heart Cookies

makes 14

ingredients

200 g/7 oz plain flour,
plus extra for dusting

100 g/3½ oz unsalted butter,
diced

100 g/3½ oz caster sugar

1 egg, lightly beaten

½ tsp vanilla extract

icing

1 large egg white,
lightly beaten

225 g/8 oz icing sugar, sifted

a few drops of warm water,
if needed

pink food colouring paste

1. Sift the flour into a large bowl. Add the diced butter and rub into the flour until the mixture resembles fine breadcrumbs. Stir in the sugar followed by the egg and vanilla extract and mix to form a crumbly dough.

2. Gather together the dough with your hands and gently knead on a lightly floured surface until smooth. Wrap the dough in clingfilm and chill in the refrigerator for 1 hour. Line two large baking sheets with baking paper.

3. Unwrap the dough and roll out on a lightly floured surface to a thickness of 5 mm/¼ inch. Using 7-cm/2¾-inch and 3-cm/1¼-inch heart-shaped cutters, stamp out 14 large and 14 small cookies, re-rolling the dough as necessary. Place on the prepared baking sheets and chill in the refrigerator for a further 20 minutes. Preheat the oven to 180°C/350°F/Gas Mark 4.

4. Bake in the preheated oven for 10–12 minutes, or until very pale golden around the edges. Leave to cool on the baking sheets for a few minutes, then transfer to wire racks to cool completely.

5. To make the icing, place the egg white in a large bowl. Gradually beat in the icing sugar to make a smooth, thick icing. Add a few drops of warm water, if needed, to get the correct consistency. Reserve 1 tablespoon of the icing in a small bowl and cover the surface with clingfilm to prevent it from drying out.

6. Spoon one-third of the remaining icing into a separate bowl and colour it pink. Spoon into a piping bag fitted with a fine plain nozzle and pipe a thin outline around each cookie. Leave to set for 10 minutes.

7. Gently spoon a little of the white icing into the centre of one of the large cookies and ease to the piped outline with a teaspoon. Shake the cookie gently to flatten the icing and remove any air bubbles with the tip of a cocktail stick. Repeat to fill all the large cookies.

8. Pipe pink dots onto the white icing. Pipe the remaining pink icing into the small cookie hearts, easing the icing to the outline with a cocktail stick. Leave the iced cookies on a wire rack to set for 3–4 hours, or overnight. Spread the base of the small cookies with a little of the reserved white icing, then gently place on top of the large cookies. Leave to set.

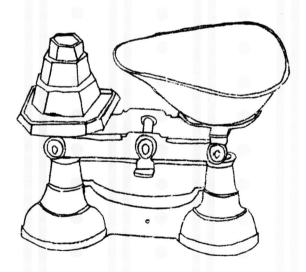

3

6

8

top tip

You can make these cookies in whatever shapes you fancy. Double decker star cookies would make the perfect Christmas gift.

Handprint Cookies

makes 20

ingredients

200 g/7 oz unsalted butter, softened

150 g/5½ oz caster sugar

1 large egg

2 tsp vanilla extract

400 g/14 oz plain flour

to decorate

1 egg white, lightly beaten or 2 tbsp cooled boiled water

edible lustre powder in the colour of your choice

1. Line two baking sheets with baking paper.

2. In a large bowl, cream the butter and sugar with an electric mixer until just coming together. Add the egg and vanilla extract and briefly whisk together.

3. Add the flour and use a wooden spoon to mix everything together to form a rough dough. Gather the dough into a ball with your hands, wrap in clingfilm and chill in the refrigerator for at least 10 minutes.

4. Unwrap the dough and roll out between two large sheets of baking paper, turning the dough occasionally until it is an even thickness of about 5 mm/¼ inch. Stamp out 20 handprint shapes using a shaped cutter or by cutting around a template, re-rolling the dough as necessary.

5. Transfer the cookies to the prepared baking sheets and chill in the refrigerator for 10 minutes. Meanwhile, preheat the oven to 180°C/350°F/Gas Mark 4.

6. Bake in the preheated oven for 15–18 minutes, or until just turning golden at the edges. Leave to cool on the baking sheets for a few minutes, then transfer to wire racks to cool completely.

7. To decorate, use a small paint brush to brush a little of the egg white over the fingertips of the cookies and sprinkle with lustre powder. Hold a small shaped cutter in place over each palm, brush a little more of the egg white inside the shape, then sprinkle with the lustre powder.

4   6   7

Quilted Cookies

makes 18

ingredients

55 g/2 oz unsalted butter, softened, plus extra for greasing

85 g/3 oz caster sugar

1 tsp finely grated orange rind

1 egg, lightly beaten

175 g/6 oz plain flour

to decorate

25 g/1 oz icing sugar, sifted

½ tsp warm water

300 g/10½ oz white ready-to-roll icing (sugar paste)

pink and blue food colouring pastes

edible silver balls

1. Place the butter, caster sugar and orange rind in a large bowl and beat together until pale and creamy. Beat in the egg, then sift in the flour and mix to form a crumbly dough. Gather together with your hands and knead lightly on a floured surface until smooth. Wrap in clingfilm and chill in the refrigerator for 30 minutes. Lightly grease two baking sheets.

2. Unwrap the dough and roll out between two large sheets of baking paper to a thickness of about 5 mm/¼ inch. Using a 7-cm/2¾-inch fluted square cutter, stamp out 18 cookies, re-rolling the dough as necessary. Place on the prepared baking sheets, spaced well apart. Chill in the refrigerator for a further 20 minutes. Preheat the oven to 190°C/375°F/Gas Mark 5.

3. Bake in the preheated oven for 10–12 minutes, or until set and very pale golden around the edges. Leave to cool on the baking sheets for a few minutes, then transfer to wire racks to cool completely.

4. Mix together the icing sugar and water to form a spreadable icing and set aside.

5. Colour half of the ready-to-roll icing pink and half blue by kneading in a little of each food colouring paste. Roll out the pink icing between two sheets of baking paper to a thickness of 3 mm/⅛ inch and, using the same square cutter, stamp out nine squares. Spread a little of the spreadable icing onto half the cookies and top with the pink squares. Repeat with the blue icing and remaining cookies.

6. Use a long, thin-bladed knife to gently score a grid pattern across the top of each cookie. Decorate with silver balls to give a quilted effect, pressing them firmly into the soft icing. Leave in a cool place until the sugar paste is firm.

2

5

5

Lollipop Swirl Cookies

makes 12

ingredients

200 g/7 oz unsalted butter, softened
150 g/5½ oz caster sugar
1 large egg
2 tsp vanilla extract
400 g/14 oz plain flour
12 lollipop sticks

royal icing

450 g/1 lb icing sugar, sifted
15 g/½ oz egg white powder
90 ml/3 fl oz water
food colouring pastes in 3 different colours of your choice

1. Line three baking sheets with baking paper.

2. In a large bowl, cream the butter and caster sugar with an electric mixer until just coming together. Add the egg and vanilla extract and briefly whisk together.

3. Add the flour and use a wooden spoon to mix everything together to form a rough dough. Gather into a ball with your hands, wrap in clingfilm and chill in the refrigerator for at least 10 minutes.

4. Unwrap the dough and roll out between two large sheets of baking paper, turning the dough occasionally until it is an even thickness of about 8 mm/⅜ inch. Stamp out about 12 circles using an 8-cm/3¼-inch plain round cutter, re-rolling the dough as necessary.

5. Transfer the cookies to the prepared baking sheets, leaving room for the lollipop sticks. Dip one end of a lollipop stick in water and then carefully insert it into the centre of the bottom of a cookie, pushing it in about halfway into the cookie. Repeat with the remaining lollipop sticks and cookies. Chill in the refrigerator for 10 minutes. Meanwhile, preheat the oven to 180°C/350°F/Gas Mark 4.

6. Bake in the preheated oven for 15–18 minutes, or until just turning golden at the edges. Leave to cool on the baking sheets for a few minutes, then transfer to wire racks to cool completely.

7. To make the royal icing, sift the icing sugar into a large mixing bowl, then add the egg white powder and water. Stir with a spoon until the icing is smooth and combined. Next, use an electric mixer to beat the mixture for 3–4 minutes, or until it becomes thick and is the texture of toothpaste.

8. Spoon a quarter of the icing into a piping bag fitted with a fine plain nozzle. Cover the remaining icing with damp kitchen paper. Carefully pipe a border around the edge of each cookie and leave to set for 10 minutes. Meanwhile, preheat the oven to 50–70°C/120–160°F or the lowest setting.

9. To make the runny or 'flood' icing, add water to the remaining icing, a drop at a time, beating between additions, until the icing is the consistency of thick Greek-style yogurt. Divide the icing evenly between four bowls and add a different food colouring to three of the bowls. Spoon each of the icings into a squeezy icing bottle or a piping bag fitted with a plain nozzle.

10. One at a time, invert a squeezy bottle of coloured icing and direct the runny icing inside the piped border of a cookie to 'flood' and fill inside the border with the icing. Next, take the squeezy bottle of white icing and, starting in the centre, pipe a spiral onto each cookie (on top of the coloured icings). Gently tap the cookies to make any air bubbles rise to the surface and pop these with a cocktail stick.

11. Return the cookies to the preheated oven to dry for about 40 minutes – they are ready when the icing is nice and hard. Transfer the cookies to a wire rack and leave to cool completely.

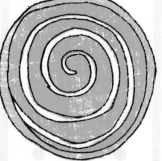

5

top tip

You need only a tiny amount of food colouring paste to give an intense colour. To avoid adding too much, dip a cocktail stick into the food colouring and stir into the icing.

CHAPTER 4
Fun & Frosted

10

10

Message Cookies

makes 30

ingredients

225 g/8 oz unsalted butter, softened

140 g/5 oz caster sugar

1 egg yolk, lightly beaten

2 tsp orange juice or orange liqueur

finely grated rind of 1 orange

280 g/10 oz plain flour

pinch of salt

icing

1 egg white

225 g/8 oz icing sugar

food colouring paste in the colour of your choice

1. Place the butter and sugar in a large bowl and beat together until light and fluffy, then beat in the egg yolk, orange juice and orange rind. Sift the flour and salt into the mixture and stir until combined. Halve the dough and shape into two balls, then wrap in clingfilm and chill in the refrigerator for 30–60 minutes.

2. Preheat the oven to 190°C/375°F/Gas Mark 5. Line two large baking sheets with baking paper.

3. Unwrap the dough and roll out to a thickness of 3 mm/$\frac{1}{8}$ inch. Depending on the occasion, stamp out appropriate shapes with cookie cutters and transfer to the prepared baking sheets, spaced well apart.

4. Bake in the preheated oven for 10–15 minutes, or until light golden brown. Leave to cool on the baking sheets for a few minutes, then transfer to wire racks to cool completely.

5. Put the egg white and icing sugar into a bowl and beat until smooth, adding a little water if necessary. Transfer two thirds of the icing to a separate bowl, then stir in a few drops of food colouring paste. Put the white icing in a piping bag fitted with a fine nozzle.

6. Spread the coloured icing over the top of the cookies using the back of a spoon. Pipe dots of the white icing around the edges of each cookie, on top of the coloured icing, and add the message of your choice. Leave to set.

5

6

6

Piñata Cookies

makes 10

ingredients

200 g/7 oz unsalted butter, softened

150 g/5 oz caster sugar

1 large egg

2 tsp vanilla extract

375 g/13 oz plain flour

25 g/1 oz cocoa powder

100 g/4 oz white chocolate, broken into pieces

175 g/6 oz small sweets of your choice

hundreds and thousands, to decorate

1. Line two baking sheets with baking paper.

2. Put the butter and sugar into a bowl and beat with an electric mixer until light and fluffy, then beat in the egg and vanilla extract. Divide the creamed mixture evenly between two bowls. Sift 200 g/7 oz of the flour into one bowl and mix together to form a rough dough. Gather into a ball with your hands, wrap in clingfilm and chill in the refrigerator for at least 10 minutes. Sift the remaining flour and the cocoa into the other bowl and mix together to make a rough dough. Gather, wrap and chill the dough as before.

3. Place one ball of dough between two sheets of baking paper and roll out to a thickness of about 5 mm/¼ inch. Repeat with the second ball of dough. Stamp out 25 cookies from each dough using a 6-cm/2½-inch plain round cutter, re-rolling the dough as necessary.

4. Transfer ten vanilla and ten cocoa cookies to the prepared baking sheets. Using a 4-cm/1½-inch plain round cutter, remove a circle from the centre of the remaining cookies. Transfer to the prepared baking sheets and chill in the refrigerator for 10 minutes. Meanwhile, preheat the oven to 180°C/350°F/Gas Mark 4.

5. Bake in the preheated oven for 15–18 minutes, or until the vanilla cookies are golden. Leave to cool on the baking sheets for a few minutes, then transfer to wire racks to cool completely.

6. To assemble, put the white chocolate in a small heatproof bowl set over a saucepan of gently simmering water and stir until melted. Remove from the heat and leave to cool for 10 minutes.

7. Spoon the cooled melted chocolate into a paper piping bag and use scissors to snip off the tip. Take a solid vanilla cookie and pipe a circle of melted chocolate around the edge, then top with a cocoa ring. Repeat this process to attach a vanilla ring and then another cocoa ring (making a total of four layers). Fill the hollow in the centre of the rings with sweets.

8. Finally, pipe melted chocolate around the edge of the uppermost cocoa ring and top with another solid vanilla cookie. Repeat to make nine more stacks the same way, but starting with a cocoa solid cookie for five of the stacks and alternating the colours as before.

9. To decorate, pipe any remaining melted chocolate in zigzags over the top of the stacks, then sprinkle with hundreds and thousands. Leave to set.

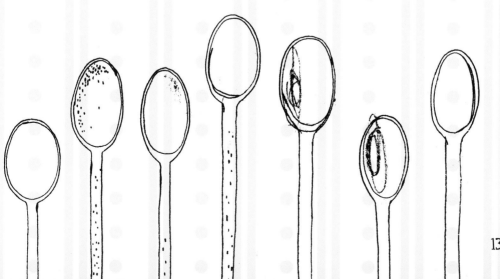

2

4

7

top tip

Instead of the melted chocolate, you could use a simple icing, made from icing sugar and water, to stick the cookie layers together.

138

Matchstick Cookies

makes 30

ingredients

70 g/2½ oz unsalted butter,
softened, plus extra
for greasing

50 g/1¾ oz caster sugar

1 tsp finely grated lemon rind

1 egg yolk

115 g/4 oz plain flour,
plus extra for dusting

1 tbsp cornflour

icing

1 tbsp egg white, lightly beaten

70 g/2½ oz icing sugar, sifted

a few drops of lemon juice

pink food colouring paste

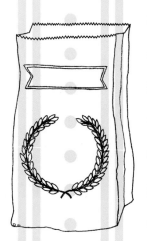

1. Place the butter, caster sugar and lemon rind in a large bowl and beat together until pale and creamy. Beat in the egg yolk, then sift in the flour and cornflour and mix to form a rough dough. Gather together with your hands and knead lightly on a floured surface until smooth. Roll into a log shape, then wrap in clingfilm and chill in the refrigerator for 45 minutes. Lightly grease two baking sheets.

2. Roll out the dough on a lightly floured surface to a thickness of about 5 mm/¼ inch. Cut into 30 thin sticks each measuring 5 mm/¼ inch wide by 9 cm/3½ inches long, re-rolling the dough as necessary. Place on the prepared baking sheets and chill in the refrigerator for a further 20 minutes. Preheat the oven to 190°C/375°F/Gas Mark 5.

3. Bake in the preheated oven for 7–9 minutes, or until pale golden. Leave to cool on the baking sheets for a few minutes, then transfer to wire racks to cool completely.

4. To make the icing, place the egg white in a bowl and gradually beat in the icing sugar and lemon juice to make a thick icing. Beat in a little pink food colouring to give a pale pink colour.

5. Gently dip one end of each matchstick cookie in the icing. Place on a wire rack with the iced ends hanging over the edge of the rack and leave to set.

top tip

For added sparkle, dip the iced ends of the cookies in pink shimmer sugar.

Fun & Frosted
CHAPTER 4

Double Heart Cookies

makes 30

ingredients

1 sachet instant latte

1½ tsp hot water

225 g/8 oz unsalted butter, softened

140 g/5 oz caster sugar

1 egg yolk, lightly beaten

250 g/9 oz plain flour

2 pinches of salt

1 tsp vanilla extract

3 tbsp cocoa powder

1. Put the instant latte into a small bowl and stir in the hot water to make a paste. Put the butter and sugar into a separate bowl and mix well with a wooden spoon, then beat in the egg yolk. Divide the mixture between two bowls. Beat the latte paste into one bowl. Sift in 140 g/5 oz of the flour and a pinch of salt into the mixture and stir. Shape the dough into a ball, wrap in clingfilm and chill in the refrigerator for 30–60 minutes.

2. Beat the vanilla extract into the other bowl, then sift in the remaining flour, the cocoa and a pinch of salt and stir. Shape the dough into a ball, wrap in clingfilm and chill as before.

3. Preheat the oven to 190°C/375°F/Gas Mark 5. Line two baking sheets with baking paper.

4. Unwrap both doughs and roll out each between two sheets of baking paper. Stamp out 15 cookies from each dough with a 7-cm/2¾-inch heart-shaped cutter and put them on the prepared baking sheets, spaced well apart. Using a 4–5-cm/1½–2-inch heart-shaped cutter, stamp out the centres of each larger heart and remove from sheets. Put a small cocoa-flavoured heart in the centre of each large coffee-flavoured heart and vice versa.

5. Bake in the preheated oven for 10–15 minutes. Leave to cool on the baking sheets for a few minutes, then transfer to wire racks to cool completely.

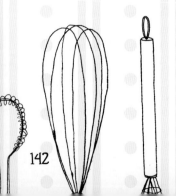

top tip

For triple heart cookies,
use three different sizes of
cookie cutters.

Fun & Frosted
CHAPTER 4

143

Moustache Cookie Pops

makes 24

ingredients

200 g/7 oz unsalted butter,
softened

150 g/5½ oz caster sugar

1 large egg

2 tsp vanilla extract

400 g/14 oz plain flour

24 lollipop sticks

edible writing pens or
writing icing, to decorate

royal icing

450 g/1 lb icing sugar, sifted

15 g/½ oz egg white powder

90 ml/3 fl oz water

1. Line two or three baking sheets with baking paper.

2. In a large bowl, cream the butter and caster sugar with an electric mixer until just coming together. Add the egg and vanilla extract and briefly whisk together. Add the flour and use a wooden spoon to mix everything together to make a rough dough. Gather into a ball with your hands, wrap in clingfilm and chill in the refrigerator for at least 10 minutes.

3. Meanwhile, draw various moustache shapes on stiff card with a pencil, then cut out to make moustache-shaped templates.

4. Roll out the dough between two large sheets of baking paper, turning the dough occasionally, until it is a thickness of about 5 mm/¼ inch. Use a knife to cut around the templates to make 24 moustache shapes, re-rolling the dough as necessary.

5. Transfer the cookies to the prepared baking sheets, leaving room for the lollipop sticks. Dip the end of a lollipop stick in water and then carefully insert it into the base of a cookie. Repeat with the remaining lollipop sticks and cookies. Chill in the refrigerator for 10 minutes. Meanwhile, preheat the oven to 180°C/350°F/Gas Mark 4.

6. Bake in the preheated oven for 15–18 minutes, or until just turning golden at the edges. Leave to cool on the baking sheets for a few minutes, then transfer to wire racks to cool completely.

7. To make the royal icing, sift the icing sugar into a large mixing bowl, then add the egg white powder and water. Stir with a spoon until the icing is smooth and combined. Next, use an electric mixer to beat the mixture for 3-4 minutes, or until it becomes thick and is the texture of toothpaste.

8. Spoon quarter of the icing into a piping bag fitted with a fine plain nozzle. Cover the remaining icing with damp kitchen paper. Carefully pipe a border around the edge of each cookie and leave to set for 10 minutes. Meanwhile, preheat the oven to 50-70°C/120-160°F or the lowest setting.

9. To make the runny or 'flood' icing, add water to the remaining icing, a drop at a time, beating between additions, until the icing is the consistency of thick Greek-style yogurt.

10. Fill a squeezy icing bottle or piping bag fitted with a plain nozzle with the runny icing. Invert the squeezy bottle and direct the runny icing inside the piped border of a cookie to 'flood' and fill inside the border with the icing. Gently tap the cookie to make any air bubbles rise to the surface and pop these with a cocktail stick. Repeat with the rest of the cookies and runny icing.

11. Return the cookies to the preheated oven for about 40 minutes – they are ready when the icing is nice and hard. Transfer the cookies to wire racks and leave to cool completely.

12. To finish, use edible writing pens or writing icing to decorate each moustache cookie and make it look nice and hairy! Leave to dry before serving.

4

top tip

Instead of using the writing pens to decorate the cookies, scatter chocolate sprinkles over the icing while it is wet for really hairy looking moustaches!

7

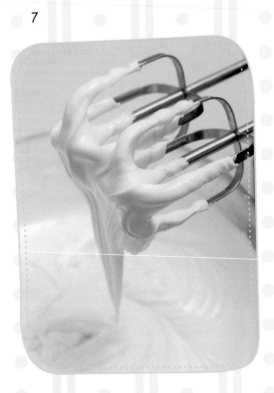

10

Tutti Frutti Whoopie Pies

makes 25

ingredients

250 g/9 oz plain flour

1 tsp bicarbonate of soda

large pinch of salt

115 g/4 oz unsalted butter, softened

150 g/5½ oz caster sugar

1 large egg, beaten

½ tsp vanilla extract

150 ml/5 fl oz buttermilk

115 g/4 oz mixed coloured glacé cherries, finely chopped

4 tbsp hundreds and thousands

marshmallow filling

225 g/8 oz white marshmallows

4 tbsp milk

a few drops of pink food colouring paste

115 g/4 oz white vegetable fat

55 g/2 oz icing sugar, sifted

1. Preheat the oven to 180°C/350°F/Gas Mark 4. Line two or three large baking sheets with baking paper. Sift the flour, bicarbonate of soda and salt into a large bowl and set aside.

2. Place the butter and caster sugar in a large bowl and beat with an electric mixer until pale and fluffy. Beat in the egg and vanilla extract followed by half the flour mixture and then the buttermilk. Stir in the rest of the flour mixture and mix until thoroughly incorporated. Stir in the glacé cherries.

3. Pipe or spoon 50 small mounds of the mixture onto the prepared baking sheets, spaced well apart.

4. Bake in the preheated oven for 9–11 minutes, until risen and just firm to the touch. Leave to cool on the baking sheets for a few minutes, then transfer to wire racks to cool completely.

5. For the filling, place the marshmallows, milk and food colouring in a heatproof bowl set over a pan of gently simmering water. Leave until the marshmallows have melted, stirring occasionally. Remove from the heat and leave to cool.

6. Place the vegetable fat and icing sugar in a bowl and beat together until smooth and creamy. Add the creamed mixture to the cooled marshmallow mixture and beat for 1–2 minutes, until fluffy.

7. To assemble, spread the filling over the flat side of half of the whoopie pies. Top with the remaining whoopie pies. Spread the hundreds and thousands on a plate and gently roll the edges of each whoopie pie in them to lightly coat.

top tip

These cute and colourful mini whoopie pies are perfect for parties.

Fun & Frosted
CHAPTER 4

Fancy Iced Spiced Cookies

makes 16

ingredients

100 g/3½ oz unsalted butter, softened, plus extra for greasing

55 g/2 oz caster sugar

1 egg, lightly beaten

225 g/8 oz plain flour, plus extra for dusting

½ tsp baking powder

2 tsp ground mixed spice

icing

1 large egg white, lightly beaten

225 g/8 oz icing sugar, sifted

a few drops of warm water, if needed

yellow and blue food colouring pastes

1. Place the butter and caster sugar in a large bowl and beat together until pale and creamy. Gradually beat in the egg, then sift in the flour, baking powder and mixed spice and mix to form a crumbly dough. Gather together with your hands and knead lightly on a floured surface until smooth. Wrap in clingfilm and chill in the refrigerator for 30 minutes. Preheat the oven to 180°C/350°F/Gas Mark 4. Lightly grease two large baking sheets.

2. Roll out the dough on a lightly floured surface to a thickness of 5 mm/¼ inch. Using a 7-cm/2¾-inch plain round cutter, stamp out 16 circles, re-rolling the dough as necessary. Transfer to the prepared baking sheets. Bake in the preheated oven for 10–12 minutes, or until pale golden. Leave to cool on the baking sheets for a few minutes, then transfer to wire racks to cool completely.

3. To make the icing, place the egg white in a large bowl. Gradually beat in the icing sugar to make a smooth, thick icing. Add a few drops of warm water, if needed, to get the correct consistency. Spoon two tablespoons of the icing into a small bowl and colour it yellow. Spoon another two tablespoons of icing into a second small bowl and colour it blue. Spoon the coloured icings into separate small paper piping bags and snip off the ends.

4. Working with one cookie at a time, spread a little of the white icing over the top, right up to the edges. While the icing is still wet, pipe parallel lines of coloured icing across the white icing. Drag the tip of a cocktail stick across the lines. Alternatively, pipe concentric circles of coloured icing on top of the white icing, then drag the tip of a cocktail stick through the icing from the centre to the edge and back again. Leave to set.

Gingerbread Men

makes 16

ingredients

450 g/1 lb plain flour,
plus extra for dusting

2 tsp ground ginger

1 tsp bicarbonate of soda

115 g/4 oz unsalted butter,
plus extra for greasing

5 tbsp golden syrup

150 g/5½ oz soft light
brown sugar

1 large egg, beaten

48 candy-coated chocolate
buttons, to decorate

royal icing

1 tbsp egg white, lightly beaten

85 g/3 oz icing sugar, sifted

a few drops of lemon juice

1. Preheat the oven to 180°C/350°F/Gas Mark 4. Lightly grease two large baking sheets. Sift the flour, ginger and bicarbonate of soda into a large bowl and set aside.

2. Put the butter, golden syrup and brown sugar into a saucepan and gently heat until syrupy. Add the flour mixture together with the egg and mix to form a firm dough.

3. Roll out the dough on a lightly floured work surface to a thickness of 8 mm/⅜ inch. Using a shaped cutter, stamp out 16 gingerbread men, re-rolling the dough as necessary. Place on the prepared baking sheets, spaced well apart.

4. Bake in the preheated oven for 10–15 minutes, until golden brown. Leave to cool on the baking sheets for a few minutes, then transfer to wire racks to cool completely.

5. To make the icing, place the egg white in a bowl and gradually beat in the icing sugar and lemon juice to make a thick icing.

6. Spoon the icing into a piping bag fitted with a fine plain nozzle and use to decorate the gingerbread men with faces and bow ties. Attach the chocolate buttons with a little of the icing. Leave to set.

2

3

6

CHAPTER 5

SOMETHING
A BIT SPECIAL

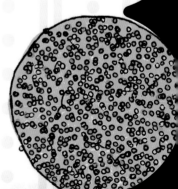

Crunchy Nut & Honey Cookie Sandwiches

makes 30

ingredients

300 g/10½ oz unsalted butter, softened

140 g/5 oz caster sugar

1 egg yolk, lightly beaten

2 tsp vanilla extract

280 g/10 oz plain flour

pinch of salt

40 g/1½ oz pine nuts, roughly chopped

85 g/3 oz icing sugar

85 g/3 oz set honey

1. Preheat the oven to 190°C/375°F/Gas Mark 5. Line two baking sheets with baking paper.

2. Put 225 g/8 oz of the butter and the caster sugar into a bowl and mix well with a wooden spoon, then beat in the egg yolk and vanilla extract. Sift the flour and salt into the mixture and stir until thoroughly combined.

3. Scoop up tablespoons of the dough and roll into balls. Put half of them on one of the prepared baking sheets, spaced well apart, and flatten gently. Spread out the pine nuts in a shallow dish and dip one side of the remaining dough balls into them, then place on the other baking sheet, nut side uppermost, and flatten gently.

4. Bake in the preheated oven for 10–15 minutes, until light golden brown. Leave to cool on the baking sheets for a few minutes, then transfer to wire racks to cool completely.

5. Beat the remaining butter with the icing sugar and honey until creamy and thoroughly mixed. Spread the honey mixture over the plain cookies and top with the nut-coated cookies.

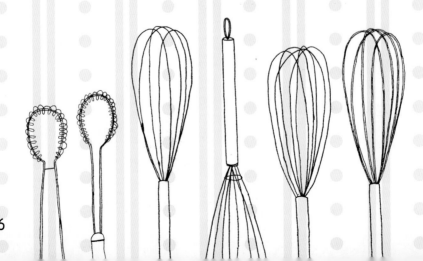

top tip

Try using pecan nuts and maple syrup instead of the pine nuts and honey.

Something a Bit Special
CHAPTER 5

Alphabet Cookies

makes 24

ingredients

200 g/7 oz unsalted butter, softened

150 g/5½ oz caster sugar

1 large egg

2 tsp vanilla extract

400 g/14 oz plain flour

buttercream

75 g/2¾ oz icing sugar

25 g/1 oz cocoa powder

50 g/1¾ oz unsalted butter, softened

1–2 tbsp milk

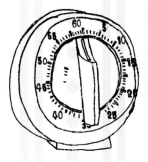

1. In a large bowl, cream the butter and caster sugar with an electric mixer until just coming together. Add the egg and vanilla extract and briefly whisk. Add the flour and use a wooden spoon to mix together to form a rough dough. Gather into a ball with your hands, wrap in clingfilm and chill in the refrigerator for at least 10 minutes. Line two large baking sheets with baking paper.

2. Unwrap the dough and roll out between two large sheets of baking paper, turning the dough occasionally until it is a thickness of about 5 mm/ ¼ inch. Using a 6-cm/2½-inch plain round cutter, stamp out 48 circles, re-rolling the dough as necessary.

3. Transfer the cookies to the prepared baking sheets. Next, stamp out letter shapes from half of the cookies (so you end up with 24 round shapes and 24 letter shapes). Chill in the refrigerator for 10 minutes. Meanwhile, preheat the oven to 180°C/350°F/Gas Mark 4.

4. Bake in the preheated oven for 15–18 minutes, or until just turning golden at the edges. Leave to cool on the baking sheets for a few minutes, then transfer to wire racks to cool completely.

5. To make the buttercream, sift the icing sugar and cocoa into a large bowl, then add the butter and milk. Using an electric mixer, whisk the ingredients together until combined, smooth and fluffy.

6. Sandwich the cookies together with the buttercream, spreading it on the base of the plain cookies and then topping each with a letter cookie. Leave to set before serving.

3

5

6

Rainbow Swirl Cookies

makes 28

ingredients

225 g/8 oz unsalted butter, softened, plus extra for greasing

150 g/5½ oz caster sugar

1 egg yolk

1 tsp vanilla extract

280 g/10 oz plain flour, plus extra for dusting

yellow, red and blue food colouring pastes

1 tbsp egg white, lightly beaten

1. Place the butter and sugar in a large bowl and beat together until pale and creamy. Beat in the egg yolk and vanilla extract, then sift in the flour and mix to form a soft dough. Knead lightly on a floured surface until smooth.

2. Divide the dough into three equal-sized pieces. Knead some yellow food colouring into one third, adding extra flour to prevent the dough from getting too sticky. Colour the other two pieces of dough red and blue in the same way. Shape each coloured dough into a 15 cm/6 inch long log and wrap in clingfilm. Chill in the refrigerator for 1 hour.

3. Unwrap the dough and roll out each piece on a floured surface to form a rectangle measuring about 20 x 25 cm/8 x 10 inches. Carefully lift and place the rectangles of dough on top of each other. Lightly brush the top with egg white, then roll up tightly from one long side like a Swiss roll. Wrap in clingfilm and chill for 40–50 minutes, or until very firm.

4. Preheat the oven to 180°C/350°F/Gas Mark 4. Grease two large baking sheets.

5. Unwrap the dough and cut into 28 slices, each about 8 mm/⅜ inch thick. Place on the prepared baking sheets, spaced well apart.

6. Bake in the preheated oven for 10–12 minutes, or until just firm. Leave to cool on the baking sheets for a few minutes, then transfer to wire racks to cool completely.

Stained Glass Window Cookies

makes 25

ingredients

350 g/12 oz plain flour,
plus extra for dusting

pinch of salt

1 tsp bicarbonate of soda

100 g/3½ oz unsalted butter

175 g/6 oz caster sugar

1 large egg

1 tsp vanilla extract

4 tbsp golden syrup

50 boiled fruit sweets
(about 250 g/9 oz)

1. Sift the flour, salt and bicarbonate of soda into a large bowl, add the butter and rub it in until the mixture resembles breadcrumbs. Stir in the sugar. Place the egg, vanilla extract and golden syrup in a separate bowl and whisk together. Pour into the flour mixture and mix to form a smooth dough. Shape the dough into a ball, wrap in clingfilm and chill in the refrigerator for 30 minutes.

2. Preheat the oven to 180°C/350°F/Gas Mark 4. Line two large baking sheets with baking paper.

3. Unwrap the sweets, separate out into the different colours and roughly chop. Set aside.

4. Unwrap the dough and roll out on a lightly floured work surface to a thickness of 5 mm/¼ inch. Using a 7-cm/2¾-inch plain round cutter, stamp out 25 circles, re-rolling the dough as necessary.

5. Transfer the cookies to the prepared baking sheets and stamp out shapes from the centres of the cookies. Fill the holes with the chopped sweets.

6. Bake in the preheated oven for 10–12 minutes, or until the sweets are melted. Leave to cool on the baking sheets until the centres have hardened.

Cookies & Cream Sandwiches

makes 15

ingredients

125 g/4½ oz unsalted butter,
softened

75 g/2¾ oz icing sugar

115 g/4 oz plain flour

40 g/1½ oz cocoa powder

½ tsp ground cinnamon

filling

125 g/4½ oz plain chocolate,
broken into pieces

50 ml/2 fl oz double cream

1. Preheat the oven to 160°C/325°F/Gas Mark 3. Line two large baking sheets with baking paper.

2. Place the butter and icing sugar in a large bowl and beat together until light and fluffy. Sift the flour, cocoa and cinnamon into the mixture and mix to form a dough.

3. Place the dough between two sheets of baking paper and roll out to a thickness of 3 mm/⅛ inch. Stamp out 30 circles using a 6-cm/2½-inch plain round cutter, re-rolling the dough as necessary. Transfer to the prepared baking sheets.

4. Bake in the preheated oven for 15 minutes, or until firm to the touch. Leave to cool on the baking sheets for a few minutes, then transfer to wire racks to cool completely.

5. Meanwhile, make the filling. Place the chocolate and cream in a saucepan and heat gently until the chocolate has melted. Stir until smooth. Leave to cool, then chill in the refrigerator for 2 hours, or until firm. Sandwich the biscuits together in pairs with a spoonful of the filling.

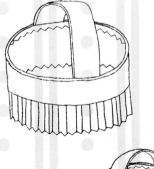

Apple Spice Cookies

makes 15

ingredients

225 g/8 oz unsalted butter, softened

140 g/5 oz caster sugar

1 egg yolk, lightly beaten

2 tsp apple juice

280 g/10 oz plain flour

½ tsp ground cinnamon

½ tsp mixed spice

pinch of salt

100 g/3½ oz ready-to-eat dried apple, finely chopped

filling

1 tbsp caster sugar

1 tbsp custard powder

125 ml/4 fl oz milk

5 tbsp apple sauce

1. Place the butter and sugar in a large bowl and beat together until light and fluffy, then beat in the egg yolk and apple juice. Sift the flour, cinnamon, mixed spice and salt into the mixture. Add the apple and stir until combined. Halve the dough and shape into two balls, then wrap in clingfilm and chill in the refrigerator for 30–60 minutes.

2. Preheat the oven to 190°C/375°F/Gas Mark 5. Line two large baking sheets with baking paper.

3. Unwrap the dough and roll out between two sheets of baking paper. Stamp out 30 cookies using a 5-cm/2-inch fluted square cutter and place them on the prepared baking sheets, spaced well apart.

4. Bake in the preheated oven for 10–15 minutes, or until light golden brown. Leave to cool on the baking sheets for a few minutes, then transfer to wire racks to cool completely.

5. To make the filling, mix together the sugar, custard powder and milk in a saucepan. Bring to the boil, stirring constantly, and cook until thickened. Remove from the heat and stir in the apple sauce. Cover the surface with clingfilm and leave to cool.

6. Sandwich the cookies together in pairs with a spoonful of the cooled filling.

top tip
Omit the filling and dip the cookies in melted white chocolate instead.

Mint Cookies with White Chocolate Ganache

makes 15

ingredients

225 g/8 oz unsalted butter, softened

140 g/5 oz caster sugar

1 egg yolk, lightly beaten

2 tsp vanilla extract

280 g/10 oz plain flour

pinch of salt

100 g/3½ oz chocolate mint sticks, finely chopped

icing sugar, for dusting

white chocolate ganache

2 tbsp double cream

100 g/3½ oz white chocolate, broken into pieces

1. Place the butter and caster sugar in a large bowl and beat together until light and fluffy, then beat in the egg yolk and vanilla extract. Sift the flour and salt into the mixture, add the chocolate sticks and stir until combined. Halve the dough and shape into two balls, then wrap in clingfilm and chill in the refrigerator for 30–60 minutes.

2. Preheat the oven to 190°C/375°F/Gas Mark 5. Line two large baking sheets with baking paper.

3. Unwrap the dough and roll out between two sheets of baking paper. Stamp out 30 cookies with a 6-cm/2½-inch fluted round cutter and place them on the prepared baking sheets, spaced well apart.

4. Bake in the preheated oven for 10–15 minutes, or until light golden brown. Leave to cool on the baking sheets for a few minutes, then transfer to wire racks to cool completely.

5. To make the ganache, pour the cream into a saucepan, add the chocolate and melt over a low heat, stirring occasionally, until smooth. Leave to cool, then chill in the refrigerator until the mixture has a spreadable consistency.

6. Spread the ganache over half the cookies and top with the remaining cookies, then dust with icing sugar.

top tip

Replace the white chocolate in the ganache with plain mint chocolate.

Marshmallow Cookie Sandwiches

makes 20

ingredients

marshmallow

sunflower oil, for greasing

1 tbsp cornflour

1 tbsp icing sugar

200 ml/7 fl oz cold water

450 g/1 lb granulated sugar

100 ml/3½ fl oz hot water

25 g/1 oz powdered gelatine

2 large egg whites

1 tsp vanilla extract

cookies

115 g/4 oz unsalted butter, softened, plus extra for greasing

55 g/2 oz caster sugar

1 egg yolk

175 g/6 oz plain flour, plus extra for dusting

250 g/9 oz plain chocolate, broken into pieces

1. Lightly oil a 23 x 33-cm/9 x 13-inch Swiss roll tin. Line the base and two short sides with baking paper then lightly oil the paper.

2. Sift the cornflour and icing sugar into a bowl. Use a little of this mixture to dust the lined tin, tapping it firmly so the mixture coats the base and sides completely.

3. Put the cold water and granulated sugar into a small, deep saucepan. Heat gently, stirring constantly with a wooden spoon, until the sugar has dissolved. Bring the syrup to the boil and boil, without stirring, for about 5 minutes, until the mixture reaches around 120°C/248°F on a sugar thermometer (the firm ball stage).

4. Meanwhile, put the hot water into a small bowl, sprinkle over the gelatine and stir until dissolved and the liquid is clear. Put the egg whites into the bowl of a free-standing electric mixer and whisk until they hold stiff peaks.

5. When the syrup has reached the correct temperature, remove from the heat and add the gelatine mixture – it will fizz and bubble. Leave to stand for a few seconds, then slowly pour the syrup into a large, heatproof jug (take care, because the mixture will be extremely hot).

6. Switch on the mixer on low speed and gradually add the hot syrup in a slow, thin stream, whisking constantly. When all the syrup has been added, increase the speed to high and whisk for 10 minutes, until the mixture is very thick and glossy and leaves a thick trail on the surface when the whisk is lifted. Whisk in the vanilla extract.

7. Pour the mixture into the prepared tin and gently level the surface. Lightly dust the top with a little of the cornflour mixture. Leave to set, uncovered, in a cool dry place for 3–4 hours.

8. Meanwhile, make the cookies. Put the butter and caster sugar into a bowl and beat with an electric mixer until pale and creamy. Beat in the egg yolk, then sift in the flour and mix to form a soft dough. Knead lightly until smooth, then wrap in clingfilm and chill in the refrigerator for 45 minutes. Grease two large baking sheets.

9. Unwrap the dough and roll out thinly on a lightly floured surface. Use a 6-cm/ 2½-inch cloud-shaped cutter to stamp out 40 cookies, re-rolling the dough as necessary. Place on the prepared baking sheets and chill in the refrigerator for 30 minutes. Preheat the oven 180°C/350°F/Gas Mark 4.

10. Bake in the preheated oven for 10–12 minutes, or until pale golden. Leave to cool on the baking sheets for a few minutes, then transfer to wire racks to cool completely.

11. Put the chocolate into a heatproof bowl set over a saucepan of gently simmering water and stir until melted. Remove from the heat and leave to cool for 10 minutes. Dip one side of each cookie in the cooled melted chocolate, then place on a wire rack set over a baking sheet. Chill in the refrigerator until set.

12. To assemble the sandwich cookies, run the tip of a lightly greased knife along the unlined sides of the tin to release the marshmallow. Using the lining paper, gently lift out the marshmallow sheet and slide onto a chopping board.

13. Wipe clean and lightly grease the cloud cutter and use to stamp out 20 cloud shapes, washing, drying and re-greasing the cutter frequently. Toss all the cloud shapes in the remaining cornflour mixture. Sandwich each marshmallow between two of the chocolate-coated cookies.

10

11

13

Ice Cream Cookie Sandwiches

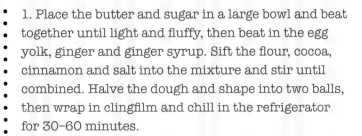

makes 30

ingredients

225 g/8 oz unsalted butter, softened

140 g/5 oz caster sugar

1 egg yolk, lightly beaten

2 tbsp finely chopped stem ginger, plus 2 tsp syrup from the jar

250 g/9 oz plain flour

25 g/1 oz cocoa powder

½ tsp ground cinnamon

pinch of salt

450 ml/15 fl oz ice cream

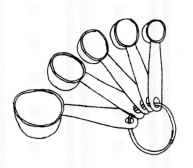

1. Place the butter and sugar in a large bowl and beat together until light and fluffy, then beat in the egg yolk, ginger and ginger syrup. Sift the flour, cocoa, cinnamon and salt into the mixture and stir until combined. Halve the dough and shape into two balls, then wrap in clingfilm and chill in the refrigerator for 30–60 minutes.

2. Preheat the oven to 190°C/375°F/Gas Mark 5. Line two large baking sheets with baking paper.

3. Unwrap the dough and roll out between two sheets of baking paper. Using a 6-cm/2½-inch fluted round cutter, stamp out 60 cookies and place them on the prepared baking sheets, spaced well apart.

4. Bake in the preheated oven for 10–15 minutes, or until light golden brown. Leave to cool on the baking sheets for a few minutes, then transfer to wire racks to cool completely.

5. Remove the ice cream from the freezer about 15 minutes before serving to allow it to soften. Put a generous scoop of ice cream on half the cookies and top with the remaining cookies. Press together gently so that the filling spreads to the edges. If not serving immediately, wrap the cookies individually in foil and store in the freezer.

top tip
Omit the stem ginger and syrup and add 1 teaspoon of peppermint extract instead.

Jam Sandwich Cookies

makes 18

ingredients

175 g/6 oz plain flour,
plus extra for dusting

100 g/3½ oz unsalted butter,
diced, plus extra for greasing

100 g/3½ oz caster sugar

1 egg, lightly beaten

½ tsp vanilla extract

filling

70 g/2½ oz unsalted butter,
softened

½ tsp vanilla extract

140 g/5 oz icing sugar, sifted

2 tbsp strawberry jam

1. Sift the flour into a large bowl. Add the diced butter and rub it into the flour with your fingertips until the mixture resembles fine breadcrumbs. Stir in the caster sugar followed by the egg and vanilla extract and mix to form a crumbly dough. Gather together with your hands and knead lightly until smooth.

2. Roll the dough into an 18 cm/7 inch long log and wrap in clingfilm. Shape the log into a square by smoothing with your hands and tapping firmly on a work surface. Use your finger and thumb to pinch the sides of the log to resemble a loaf of bread. Chill in the refrigerator for 1 hour 30 minutes, or until the dough is very firm (re-shaping the dough after 30 minutes).

3. Preheat the oven to 180°C/350°F/Gas Mark 4. Grease two large baking sheets.

4. Unwrap the dough and, using a thin-bladed knife, slice into 36 slices (each about 5 mm/¼ inch thick). Transfer to the prepared baking sheets.

5. Bake in the preheated oven for 10–12 minutes, or until very pale golden around the edges. Leave to cool on the baking sheets for a few minutes, then transfer to wire racks to cool completely.

6. For the filling, place the butter and vanilla extract in a bowl and gradually beat in the icing sugar until smooth and creamy. Sandwich the cookies together in pairs with the buttercream and jam.

4

5

6

Something a Bit Special
CHAPTER 5

Chocolate & Ginger Chequerboard Cookies

makes 30

ingredients

225 g/8 oz unsalted butter, softened

140 g/5 oz caster sugar

1 egg yolk, lightly beaten

2 tsp vanilla extract

280 g/10 oz plain flour

pinch of salt

1 tsp ground ginger

1 tbsp finely grated orange rind

1 tbsp cocoa powder

1 egg white, lightly beaten

1. Put the butter and sugar into a bowl and mix well with a wooden spoon, then beat in the egg yolk and vanilla extract. Sift the flour and salt into the mixture and stir until thoroughly combined.

2. Divide the dough in half. Add the ginger and orange rind to one half and mix well. Shape the dough into a 15 cm/6 inch long log. Flatten the sides and top to square off the log and make it 5 cm/2 inches high. Wrap in clingfilm and chill in the refrigerator for 30–60 minutes. Add the cocoa to the other half of the dough and mix well. Shape into a flattened log as before, wrap in clingfilm and chill in the refrigerator for 30–60 minutes.

3. Unwrap the dough and cut each log lengthways into three slices. Cut each slice lengthways into three strips. Brush the strips with egg white and stack them in threes, alternating the flavours, to make two chequered log shapes. Wrap in clingfilm and chill for 30–60 minutes.

4. Preheat the oven to 190°C/375°F/Gas Mark 5. Line two baking sheets with baking paper.

5. Unwrap the logs and cut into slices with a sharp, serrated knife. Transfer the cookies to the prepared baking sheets, spaced well apart.

6. Bake in the preheated oven for 12–15 minutes, until firm. Leave to cool on the baking sheets for a few minutes, then transfer to wire racks to cool completely.

top tip

Create colourful effects by adding food colouring to the dough instead of cocoa.

Rainbow Slice Cookies

makes 20

ingredients

200 g/7 oz unsalted butter, softened

150 g/5½ oz caster sugar

1 large egg

1 tsp vanilla extract

400 g/14 oz plain flour

red, orange, yellow, green, blue and purple food colouring pastes

to decorate

100 g/3½ oz white chocolate, broken into pieces

hundreds and thousands

1. Line two baking sheets with baking paper.

2. In a large bowl, cream the butter and sugar with an electric mixer until just coming together. Add the egg and vanilla extract and briefly whisk together. Add the flour and use a wooden spoon to mix everything together to form a rough dough.

3. Gather the dough into a ball with your hands, then divide it into six equal-sized portions. Knead a different food colouring into each portion of dough, kneading each one on a clean surface so the colours don't merge. Wrap each portion of coloured dough in clingfilm and chill in the refrigerator for at least 10 minutes.

4. Unwrap the dough and roll out each portion between two large sheets of baking paper, turning the dough occasionally until it is an even thickness of about 8 mm/⅜ inch and forms a rectangle measuring 20 x 10 cm/8 x 4 inches. Stack up all the rolled-out rectangles of coloured dough, one on top of another, then trim the edges so that you have a neat stack.

5. Slice the stack in half widthways to make two 10 x 10-cm/4 x 4-inch squares. Cut each square into about ten slices with each cookie measuring about 10 x 4.5 cm/4 x 1¾ inches.

6. Transfer the cookies to the prepared baking sheets. Chill in the refrigerator for 10 minutes. Meanwhile, preheat the oven to 180°C/350°F/Gas Mark 4.

7. Bake in the preheated oven for 15–18 minutes, or until just turning golden at the edges. Leave the cookies on the baking sheets to cool completely.

8. To decorate, put the chocolate in a small heatproof bowl set over a saucepan of gently simmering water and stir until melted and smooth. Remove from the heat and leave to cool slightly. Dip one end of each cookie into the melted chocolate and place back on the baking paper, then sprinkle with hundreds and thousands and leave to set.

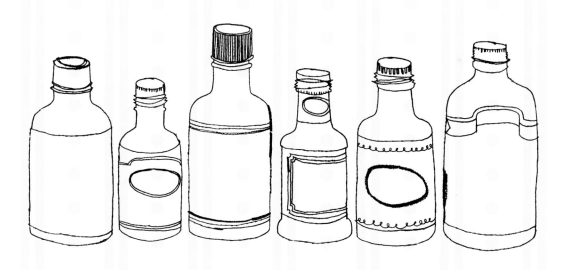

4

top tip

These bright colours can be easily achieved with natural food colourings, available online and from specialist kitchen shops.

5

8

Red Velvet Cookies

makes 20

ingredients

115 g/4 oz unsalted butter, softened

200 g/7 oz caster sugar

1 large egg, lightly beaten

1 tsp vanilla extract

½ tsp white wine vinegar

1½ tsp red liquid food colouring

225 g/8 oz plain flour

2 tbsp cocoa powder

¾ tsp baking powder

pinch of salt

85 g/3 oz white chocolate, broken into pieces

1. Preheat the oven to 190°C/375°F/Gas Mark 5. Line two large baking sheets with baking paper.

2. Place the butter and sugar in a large bowl and beat together until pale and creamy. Gradually beat in the egg, followed by the vanilla extract, vinegar and food colouring. Sift in the flour, cocoa, baking powder and salt. Stir until thoroughly blended to form a soft dough.

3. Shape the dough into 20 balls, each about the size of a golf ball. Place on the prepared baking sheets, spaced well apart, and flatten each one with your fingers.

4. Bake in the preheated oven for 10–12 minutes, or until just risen and set. Leave to cool on the baking sheets for a few minutes, then transfer to wire racks to cool completely.

5. Place the chocolate in a heatproof bowl set over a pan of gently simmering water and stir until melted and smooth. Spoon into a paper piping bag and snip off the end. Pipe zig-zag lines of chocolate over each cookie. Leave to set.

Rainbow Sprinkle Sugar Cookies

makes 18

ingredients

100 g/3½ oz unsalted butter, softened, plus extra for greasing

70 g/2½ oz caster sugar

100 g/3½ oz plain flour, plus extra for dusting

50 g/1¾ oz cornflour

1–2 tbsp milk

4 tbsp hundreds and thousands

1. Place the butter and sugar in a large bowl and beat together with an electric mixer until pale and creamy. Sift in the flour and cornflour and mix to form a crumbly dough. Gather together with your hands and knead lightly on a floured surface until smooth. Wrap in clingfilm and chill in the refrigerator for 30 minutes.

2. Preheat the oven to 180°C/350°F/Gas Mark 4. Grease two large baking sheets.

3. Unwrap the dough and roll out between two large sheets of baking paper to a thickness of 5 mm/¼ inch. Using a 6-cm/2½-inch fluted round cutter, stamp out 18 cookies, re-rolling the dough as necessary.

4. Transfer the cookies to the prepared baking sheets. Brush the tops lightly with the milk and sprinkle liberally with the hundreds and thousands, pressing down gently with your fingertips.

5. Bake in the preheated oven for 10–12 minutes, or until pale golden. Leave to cool on the baking sheets for a few minutes, then transfer to wire racks to cool completely.

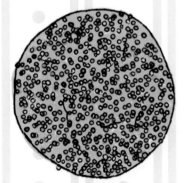

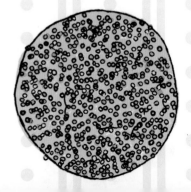

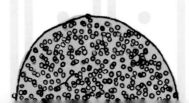

1

1

3

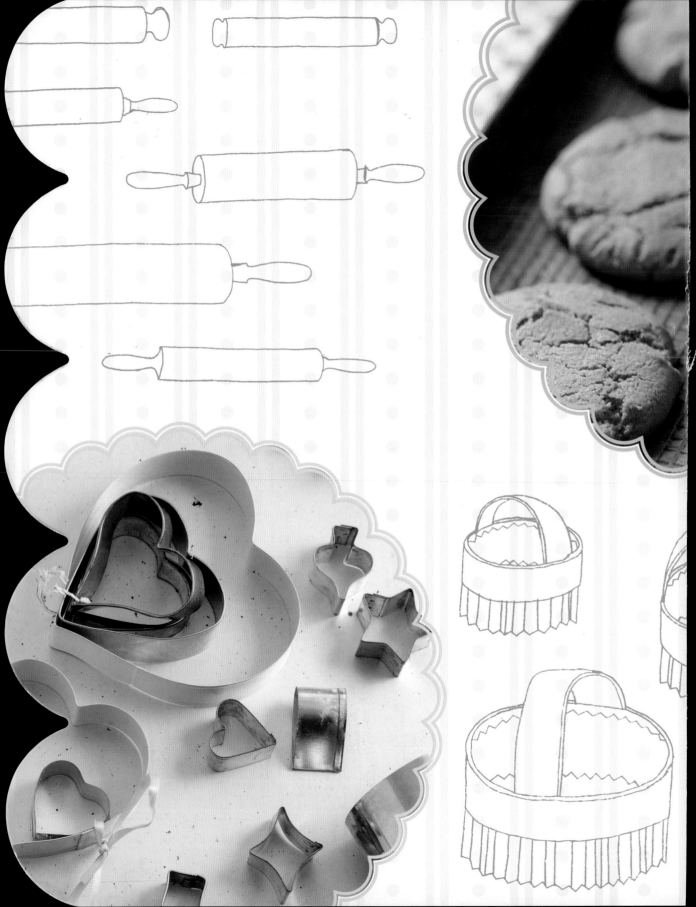

This edition published by Parragon Books Ltd in 2014
LOVE FOOD is an imprint of Parragon Books Ltd

Parragon Books Ltd
Chartist House
15–17 Trim Street
Bath BA1 1HA, UK
www.parragon.com/lovefood

ISBN 978-1-4723-4053-5

Printed in China

New recipes by Angela Drake
Additional photography by Ian Garlick
Illustrations by Charlotte Farmer

Notes for the Reader

This book uses both metric and imperial measurements. Follow the same
units of measurement throughout; do not mix metric and imperial. All spoon
measurements are level: teaspoons are assumed to be 5 ml, and tablespoons
are assumed to be 15 ml. Unless otherwise stated, milk is assumed to be full
fat, eggs and individual vegetables are medium, and pepper is freshly ground
black pepper. Unless otherwise stated, all root vegetables should be peeled prior
to using.

Garnishes, decorations and serving suggestions are all optional and not
necessarily included in the recipe ingredients or method. The times given
are an approximate guide only. Preparation times differ according to the
techniques used by different people and the cooking times may also vary from
those given. Optional ingredients, variations or serving suggestions have not
been included in the time calculations.